Gail Richards
286-4432.

P9-EDU-376

Taking Leave of God

DON CUPITT

TAKING LEAVE OF GOD

Man's last and highest parting occurs when,
for God's sake, he takes leave of God.
Eckhart: Sermon, *Qui audit me*

SCM PRESS LTD

© Don Cupitt 1980

All rights reserved. No part of this publication may be
reproduced, stored in a retrieval system, or transmitted, in
any form or by any means, electrical, mechanical,
photocopying, recording or otherwise, without the prior
permission of the publisher, SCM Press Ltd.

334 01596 0

First published 1980
by SCM Press Ltd
58 Bloomsbury Street, London WC1
Third impression 1981

Photoset by Input Typesetting Ltd
and printed in Great Britain by
Billing and Sons Ltd
Guildford, London, Oxford, Worcester

To my parents

AUGUSTANA UNIVERSITY COLLEGE
LIBRARY

Contents

	Preface	ix
1	Introductory: The Spirituality of Radical Freedom	1
2	The Decline of Objective Theism	15
3	The Charge of Reductionism	34
4	Creation and Theological Realism	46
5	Worship and Theological Realism	56
6	Doctrine and Disinterestedness	70
7	The Meaning of God	84
8	How Real Should God Be?	98
9	Is the Religious Ideal Attainable?	108
10	Faith as an Act of the Will	122
11	The Justification of Faith	140
12	The Triumph of the Religious Consciousness	156
13	Conclusion	163
	Notes	168
	Index of Names	173

Preface

Modern people increasingly demand autonomy, the power of legis-lating for oneself. They are no longer satisfied with lives that are almost wholly determined by external limitations, powers and au-thorities. As they put it, they want to live their own lives, which means making one's own rules, steering a course through life of one's own choice, thinking for oneself, freely expressing oneself and choosing one's own destiny.

In philosophy there is a classic argument to the effect that unless we claim and exercise this radical kind of freedom we are not being truly moral at all. A life lived in resigned acceptance of limitation and in passive obedience to God and tradition does not deserve to be called a moral life. I must appropriate, internalize and truly make my own the standards I live by. Merely to carry out someone else's instructions is not in itself morally admirable at all; no, not even if the one I obey is a good God. If I do obey a good God whose commands are good, my obedience is only meritorious in so far as I freely and rationally judge for myself that God's com-mands are intrinsically good and deserving of adoption as princi-ples of conduct, so that I would freely choose to obey them in any case whether God commanded them or not.

There is no goodness without radical freedom, and within the idea of radical freedom there are at least three strands, each vital. First, I must have the freedom of action I need if I am to follow the course of life and habits of action that will make me the person I want to be; secondly, I must be autonomous in the sense of being able to make my own rules and impose them upon myself; and thirdly, the morality I actually adopt must itself be autonomous in the secondary sense of being intrinsically authoritative. If it derived its authority from another I could not fully adopt and internalize it without becoming dependent upon that other, and so forfeiting my freedom.

Of course it is possible that the teaching of the Communist Party, or of Islam, or of the Catholic Church is true morality, such as I would do right to adopt and take as my guide. But even so, blind faith and blind obedience are morally wrong. I must at least be a *critical* follower of the party line, judging for myself on each occasion that the line being handed out is good in itself. Obedience as such is not a morally good thing. Prudent, maybe – but not morally good.

So the morality of a free man who is nobody's servant consists in a body of principles, ideals and values which are intrinsically good and deserving of adoption. In making them his own the free man does not lose his freedom but exercises it. Nor will his morality be arbitrary or subjective. Not at all. For a morality that deserves to be adopted must be rational, consistent and impartial. That being so, we can begin to see how a society of autonomous persons might be possible. Each chooses his own ethic, but in so far as they each recognize that morality has to be consistent and impartial, a public socially-agreed morality will tend to emerge as the product of all their separate choices. Hence the possibility of a fully free society, a liberal democratic republic, the best kind of society.

The demand for radical freedom and the moral attractiveness of the ideal of autonomy are very strong indeed, and have been so for two centuries. No doubt we have not yet achieved radical freedom in practice very well, but we think of ourselves as fitted for it. A human being is mostly made of ideals and hopes. Today everyone wishes to be his own master and captain of his own soul, and that splendid ideal determines how we think of ourselves and what we hope for. We are irreversibly committed to it because in these matters there is no going back. Once one has fully understood that it is possible to be the captain of one's own soul, then the ideal is established in one and has thereafter an unshakeable authority. I may seem to be trapped in various physical, economic and social necessities, but it does not matter: I know what freedom is, and that is three-quarters of the battle.

Perhaps we are like former colonial territories which used to be governed from outside but now have won a precarious independence. Relics of the former colonial days still lie about the place – statues of the great, churches, educational institutions, place names, and the language that was taught us by our former masters. There is controversy about these relics, some urging that they be swept away and others prizing them as a link with the past. Either way, the fact remains that the old heteronomous or external ruling

authority has been broken and cannot be restored. Not even the
most nostalgic conservatives seriously suppose it is coming back.
On the contrary, they will in practice be just as quick as anyone
else to sniff out and denounce any signs of real neo-colonialism.
The colonial period was very valuable as a time of education, a
transitional period, but it is now over.

In this way there is an analogy between the residual presence of
traditional religion in our modern autonomous psyches and the
residual presence of the former colonial power in a newly independent country. It is true that there is a good deal of residual heteronomous religion about still in people's psyches. We may like to
have it around, rather as many people find antique furnishings and
decor comfortable in their homes and hostelries, but the fact remains that we are not going to be recolonized. The old kind of
religion, a thoroughly heteronomous external control-system, is
gone and swept away by history. It is not merely that people would
sharply resent any serious attempt to reimpose it, but rather that
it is impossible to reimpose it. Having attained autonomous consciousness, I cannot knowingly revert to a condition in which a bit
of my consciousness is hived off and becomes the awesome, inscrutable will of God that directs my course through life. In the
age of autonomous morality and consciousness you can only have
heteronomous religion as a kind of affectation. I have noticed for
some years that many of my Christian friends who profess heteronomous faith feel obliged to make little jokes about it. If misfor-
tune strikes them they say jokingly that God must be annoyed;
they joke about thunder and lightning as manifestations of God's
displeasure; they joke about praying for rain or for victory in some
contest or other; and although they profess in general terms to
believe in signs of God's providence and the discernment of God's
will, they laugh at the naivety of one who applies these beliefs in
a concrete and specific way to just one particular case. This
jocularity is significant. It expresses the ironical distance between
traditional religious language and the modern autonomous consciousness. When that distancing is internal to oneself one must
use humour to express it and to relieve the strain.

It is plain that religion sooner or later must come to terms with
autonomy. After all, morality has done so. Religion must surely
follow suit, and the sooner the better.

Yet how is it to be done? Hitherto it has been thought impossible
because the God and the religious institutions of Jews, Christians
and Muslims seem to be so uncompromisingly heteronomous.

Christianity in particular seems almost to identify being a religious believer with assenting to a large body of highly implausible assertions about supernatural beings and events, but all three faiths appear to lay very great emphasis on submission to a god who is conceived of as an infinite, almighty and commanding being quite distinct from the believer, who requires absolute obedience. If indeed belief in God has to take that very objectified form then the religious consciousness must be obsolete; but I hope to show that things are not as bad as that. Despite appearances, it is possible for religion to become sufficiently autonomous to return to its proper place at the leading edge of our spiritual development. The main requirements, to be explained below, are a break with our habitual theological realism, a full internalization of all religious doctrines and themes, and a recognition that it is possible autonomously to adopt religious principles and practices as intrinsically valuable.

What will the result look like? Of the great world faiths, Buddhism comes closest to what I have in mind. It exalts spirituality above theological doctrine, and emphasizes autonomy. Hence its attraction to many in the modern West, and at one point in what follows I do use the phrase 'Christian Buddhism'. The content, the spirituality and the values, are Christian; the form is Buddhist.

Another slogan which may help to clarify things is, 'Traditional Christianity is now our Old Testament', by which I mean that we now stand towards traditional realistic, mythological Christianity in the same sort of relation as Christians have always stood in towards the Old Testament. We can fairly claim to be its inheritors, and we can draw upon its language and its spiritual resources. It belongs to us and we to it. We can even 'canonize' it provided that we do not conceal from ourselves the all-important fact that there has taken place a great meaning-shift, a change of dispensation. The third dispensation, the Age of the Spirit long promised by certain visionary figures, has in a sense already begun. Unlike the old Christian era, it had no clear starting-point but has slowly phased itself in in modern times.

Over the years I have met various people who are quietly agnostic or sceptical about Christian supernatural *doctrines*, while nevertheless continuing to practise the Christian *religion* to strikingly good effect. Such a position is usually thought to be too paradoxical, too whimsical to be publicly defended because in most peoples' eyes having faith is so much a matter of holding doctrines. Yet opinion has been shifting somewhat recently, for we have come

to see that the highly ideological character of much modern Western religion is in global terms an oddity and an exception. The
time may now be ripe for a defence of the modern sceptical believer
whose religion is autonomous and critical, rather than heteronomous and dogmatic. Perhaps he is the religious man of the
future, and perhaps his faith (Buddhist in form, Christian in content) is spiritually purer and more disinterested than that of earlier
generations whose piety seems to have needed a great deal of
mythological buttressing to prop it up.

The main themes are laid out in chapter 1. Some parts of chapter
2 may be heavy going for those who are not in the trade. If so,
miss them out. And if you do not feel the pressures that have led
me to the position here described, then this book is not for you.
Do not imagine I have any interest in scandalizing the faithful.
What would be the use of that? So if you must read it, then read
it as if it were the work of one long dead who cannot be suspected
of any intention to challenge or threaten.

D. C.

Preface to Second Impression

In this second impression I have corrected a few misprints and
have removed an erroneous statement from p. 58. Otherwise the
text is unchanged, and I hope that when the dust settles it may be
seen that the early charges of 'atheism' were over-simple. The
autonomous and undogmatic kind of faith here commended may
not presuppose any objective deity, but it may yet be capable of
attaining the ultimate goal of the religious life.

D. C.

1

INTRODUCTORY:
THE SPIRITUALITY OF RADICAL FREEDOM

'I can't live with it and I can't live without it.' Such is the verdict
of many people upon traditional religious belief. They find it especially difficult to accept the objective or metaphysical side of
religion, the side that postulates and describes various supernatural
beings, powers and events. Though in many ways such beliefs are
imaginatively attractive, we have little or no reason to think them
true; they evidently belong to a bygone age, and they invite us
back into a childhood world. The universe becomes again a vast
family home in which we are destined to remain in perpetuity,
members of the younger generation under benevolent supervision.

Yet although the doctrinal side of religion may thus seem hard
to stomach and hard to credit, few people are happy to be quite
without any religious dimension to their lives. At least they would
like to retain something of a religious sense of life's meaning and
something of religious ritual, values and spirituality.

In the last generation there was for a time a fashion for elimin-
ating religious categories altogether and 'secularizing' Christianity
– that is, interpreting it in wholly non-religious terms. It was
assumed that secular science and technology, economics and politics were rapidly creating a completely non-religious world. Certainly the great religious institutions had been pushed well away
to the margins of life, and their power was still declining. But the
secularizers also made another and more questionable assumption,
for they equated religiousness with dependency and argued that
since modern people have become more autonomous – self-defining
and self-directing – they were *ipso facto* ceasing to be religious. It
was concluded that Christianity must be re-expressed solely in

terms of purely human relationships and values, because distinctively religious ways of thinking were vanishing from the world altogether.

That diagnosis now appears to have been too hasty. The equation of religiosity with dependency (typical of the Enlightenment and of Freud) is sufficiently refuted by the mention of Buddhism, which has no trace of dependency. And in the modern West it seems that religion still has a part to play even after the great religious institutions have declined and consciousness has become autonomous. Technological rationality by itself is scarcely likely to create a habitable world for us to live in, and many now regard it as a destructive force. In addition, the typically modern pressure for thoroughgoing 'liberation' can easily issue in an anarchic freedom that rejects all structure and becomes quite contentless. A freedom that is in no way directed by a spirituality does not know what to do with itself and does not know where it is going. What we need – but lack – is illustrated by the example of a creative artist. Such a person is fortunate, for as well as his spiritual freedom he also has his vocation, which in him functions like a spirituality in that it directs his freedom towards maximally productive use and expression. So he creates a series of works which are a visible spiritual biography. Happy the person whose life bears fruit in that way. Unfortunately, though many of us moderns have by now succeeded in gaining something of the artist's inner freedom or spiritual autonomy, we lack his expressive powers and so we do not bear fruit. We are liable to become barren and even desperate. We need a spirituality to direct our freedom and make it fruitful, so that human lives can gain something of the nothing-wasted integrity and completeness of a work of art. When lives are rounded off in that way, death loses its sting. But the same great historical process that has emancipated us has also gravely weakened the traditional faiths from which we used to draw our spiritual resources. When we most need a spirituality our religious institutions seem least able to provide it. Hence there is a good deal of eccentric experimentation, ransacking of the Oriental traditions and so on, for the pearl of great price is proving difficult to find.

All this suggests that we have to come to see the modern situation much as many nineteenth-century writers saw it. As they would have put it, it is vitally important to try to preserve something of the spirit of religion even though its institutional and doctrinal aspects appear to be in irreversible decay.

How is this to be done? Three converging lines of thought point towards the answer.

The first is the great theme of *internalization*, the mighty historical process by which over a period of many centuries meanings and values are withdrawn from external reality and as it were sucked into the individual subject. Thus demons are less likely now to be seen as spirit-beings 'out there', for they have turned instead into threatening, unmastered elements within the psyche. The whole moral order was formerly seen as built into external reality, as an objective, ready-made framework to live our lives in; but it is now regarded rather as something we generate from within ourselves. All the sources from which our lives are inspired, guided and nourished have in this way come to be seen as welling up within us instead of being (as they used to be) an objective pre-existent order into which we have been inserted. In the old world meanings and values came down from above, but now they come up from below. We no longer receive them; we have to create them.

Naturally, religion is deeply involved in this whole process. It is a much larger business than the Protestant Reformation, though the Reformation was clearly part of it. We might expect to find religion gradually becoming less a system of externally-imposed demands and constraints, and more a matter of inner inspiration and guidance. We might expect to see city life and the growing power of science and technology speeding up the process by which objective institutional religion gets weaker and subjective inner religion gets stronger. We might expect to see religious doctrine understood less in cosmological terms and more in terms of redemption and the transformation of the individual life. By and large, we do see all these things happening. In modern times we find less sacred meaning and mystery in the external world around us, but by way of compensation we have as it were more religiousness inside us. Religious meaning too is nowadays to be sought within us rather than from above us.

Secondly, and closely linked with this, there is the modern demand for radical spiritual *autonomy* that perhaps began as far back as the Renaissance and has by now spread to both sexes, most age-groups and all classes of society. Historically, the defenders of traditional order have stigmatized this demand as libertinism, but it continues unabated. People increasingly want to live their own lives, to make their own choices and to determine their own destinies, and they refuse to be dissuaded by the objection that their autonomy will lead only to unhappiness. On the contrary, they insist that it is better to live one's own life, even if unsuccessfully, than to live a life which is merely the acting of a part written for us by somebody else, and the principle holds even if that 'somebody else' is a god. Anyone who has tasted freedom knows that it would be a sin against one's own soul to revert to dependency.

We notice that in the process the meaning of the term 'sin' has reversed. In traditional society the affirmation of one's own radical freedom was the very essence of sin. Sin was discontent, rebellion against the existing divinely-ordered framework of life. But today obedience is sin. Above all one must not surrender one's inner integrity; and what is integrity? – It is one's *autonomy*.

How far back we can trace the idea of radical autonomy may be questioned. In such matters traditions are created retrospectively and many people are doubtless conscripted into them who did not consciously stand for the views that hindsight ascribes to them. However, one can say that this demand for radical freedom has certainly been a major force since the Enlightenment. It is often linked with voluntarism – belief in the primacy of the will – and with an anti-religious outlook. The Western church, being established, stood for a public rational order to which the individual ought to conform himself. When an individual poet or mystic declared that his own free self-expression was more important than that order he inevitably came into conflict with the church.

Yet the demand for autonomy may not necessarily be opposed either to reason or to religion. The philosopher Kant made a most impressive attempt to reconcile autonomy with rationality in the sphere of ethics. Perhaps there may be some indications in the religious tradition of how to reconcile faith with radical autonomy so that they actually complement each other rather than threaten each other?

It is clear that the two great movements that I have called *internalization* and *autonomy* are in many ways linked, and merely to put them together is to be reminded of some very old religious themes. So our third converging line of thought is the biblical idea of the *New Covenant*. Religion cannot reach its highest development so long as the divine requirement remains an objective authority external to man which tries to control him from without. Religion requires a peculiarly complete inner transformation of human nature which cannot be brought about from outside. No external pressure upon us can make us completely disinterested;

the very idea is an absurdity. No, the power that brings about my inner transformation must be fully internalized until it springs up at the very source of my own affections and will. Hence it was said that the law written on stone tablets must be changed for a law written directly in our hearts, that our hearts of stone must be changed for hearts of flesh, that we must be circumcised inwardly and that God must put his spirit into our hearts. In the New Testament it is claimed that these promises and hopes are at last fulfilled.

All this helps us to see why conservative religion of the sort that sets God authoritatively over the believer nowadays sounds as if it is spiritually backward and not fully conscious of itself. It has become an anachronism; it is spiritually behind the times. Objectifying religion is now false religion, for it no longer saves.

Consider a member of one of those authoritarian religious groups which have no critical reflection and no irony. Such a person is absorbed in his God and his belief system. To others he seems, I am sorry to say, to be slightly mad and an object of pity and ridicule. Why? – Because he is backward, 'not all there', as people say. He is not all there because he has given up his self-consciousness to the God, or the God has stolen it from him. The God is doing fine, for he is pure spirit; but the human believer is only a shell, a slave, a living tool – not all there, because the noblest part of himself has been surrendered to the God.

How can such a sad creature be saved? He must either escape from religion altogether by the standard route that leads to humanism, or, still better if he can manage it, he can reconcile spiritual self-possession with religion by achieving inner union with his God. Then he will have the highest kind of religion, a fully autonomous spirituality – but it is very rare.

If there is a way to achieve this, then God and the human individual are no longer to be thought of as two beings in apposition. God indwells the believer, enlightening his understanding, kindling his affections and enabling his will. Pressing the theme hard (as St Paul does press it), it can be said that God's spirit enters the believer so intimately that it is the divine spirit that prays within him. The love with which the believer loves God has become identical with the love God has for the believer. I and thou are no longer numerically two but a kind of resonating one.

Here then are three converging themes – the internalization of meanings and values within the human subject, the autonomy of the human spirit and the indwelling of God within the believer.

Put them together and they suggest that today we are ceasing to speak of God in cosmic or objective terms. The English Common Prayer Book of 1662 contains forms of prayer for rain and for fair weather, but who now thinks of God like that? Instead, God now belongs in the context of spirituality and the inner life.

The changeover is, as I suggest, evidently taking place for, whatever our verbal professions, in practice we have largely ceased to take seriously the idea that God controls the course of events in the physical world. If God's government be identified with the law-abidingness of the natural course of events, as in Deism, then it is redundant. It adds nothing. Alternatively, if God's action in nature be seen as a matter of extraordinary interventions, then it is well known by now that insuperable difficulties surround all attempts to identify such events and to prove that God and God alone could have caused them to occur. So there are severe problems with the traditional notions both of God's general providence and of his particular providences, and nowadays theologians put about a much vaguer doctrine, saying that the world-process, being non-deterministic, leaves scope for God to be thought of as guiding it in a very general way towards the fulfilment of his purposes; and since persons in particular are supposed to be non-deterministic, that guiding hand of God is most clearly apparent in the shaping of people's lives.[1]

The trouble is that by the time such an account of providence has taken due care to avoid superstition and animism it is left saying nothing definite. It is said that 'God makes creatures make themselves', but this says no more than that creatures make themselves. It is said that, as words like *grace* and *inspiration* make clear, religious experience has a quality of givenness about it; but as the psychologists of religion are well aware, there is no way of distinguishing between the purely natural 'givenness' of an uprush from the unconscious, and genuine God-givenness. Divine interventions are no easier to identify in psychology than they are in external nature. It is said that God is distinctively loving and that patterns of loving activity experienced by us may be ascribed to God, but how in practice can that really be distinguished from the more modest observation that Christian people are influenced by Christian ideals both in their conduct and in their interpretation of events?

So this kind of theologians' talk of providence is by now so attenuated as to be worthless. Why have the theologians attenuated it so much? They have done so largely to avoid the ugly eudae-

attenuated — ① tu make thin or slender...
② to lessen the amt, force or value)

Vacuous — emptied of or lacking content
(2) marked by or indicative of mental vacuity
or lack of ideas or intelligence
(dull - stupid)

monism of the popular idea of providence. For people talk of providence in connection with fortunate coincidences, lucky escapes and personal success, as if they really think that the universe revolves around themselves and that God's chief preoccupation is with smoothing their path through life. The air-crash survivor thanks God for his deliverance, but what of those who died? A God who schedules some to survive and some to die in a forthcoming air-crash is clearly repugnant. Who can seriously suppose that the world is run in such a way? So the theologian cannot stomach a particularist or close-up idea of providence; for him, providence is only endurable at the most general level. But then the terms have to be made so general that the idea of providence becomes vacuous for (as is pointed out below, in chapter 7) government by personal rule, however enlightened, is always in the long run morally intolerable and spiritually oppressive. Good government is government by general laws and not by personal rule. So if God is good, God must fade out, and if the theologians still wish to maintain that there is a good providence it will have to be made so general and lawlike that it disappears.

Thus it has come about that our spiritual and moral development (not to mention the development of natural science) has removed God from the control of the external world. In the first few chapters that follow I give many other arguments along similar lines, suggesting that we do not have sufficient evidence to justify objective theism, that the evidence for it that we do have cannot be sufficient to justify an unconditional religious commitment, that traditional faith is far from indissolubly wedded to theological realism, and so on.

However, the grip of theological realism on people's minds is very strong indeed. Biblical belief in God was translated into metaphysical terms by Philo of Alexandria, a contemporary of Jesus, and ever since then the metaphysical interpretation of theism has been so dominant that even today most people think there can be no faith in God without presupposing it. The philosophers are almost unanimous that the only God there can be is their god, the God of the philosophers, and that if *he* does not exist then talk of God has no useful job to do.

There has always been a minority view, and it includes many of the best names, for Tertullian, Luther, Pascal, Kierkegaard and Barth were all antimetaphysical and refused to identify the God of faith with the philosophers' God. In more recent years the psychologist C. G. Jung clearly did not believe in any objective or

eudaemonism — an ethical theory
that defines moral obligation by
reference to happiness... through a
life governed by reason rather than the
pursuit of happiness.

metaphysical God, yet towards the end of his life he would say
that he did not merely believe in God, he knew God. In his book
Honest to God and its successors, Dr John Robinson also denied
the existence of any metaphysical God 'out there'. The point he
was making was that the metaphysical expression of faith in God
was not essential but only temporary and culturally conditioned.
In the most ancient times belief in God had taken a mythological
form. From (say) Philo to the Enlightenment it had taken a metaphysical form. Now in the modern period it would again have to
be reformulated.

Both Robinson and Jung were aware that an objective God 'out
there' would be spiritually oppressive and would block man's attainment of full self-consciousness. To liberate man, God must be
internalized. But how is this to be done? Robinson and Jung seem
to make religion too immanent, too human and too little distinct
from culture. It is dangerous to identify the religious domain with
the depths of the natural psyche. Is there any way of overcoming
religious heteronomy (God's spiritually crushing *over-againstness*)
while yet maintaining the transcendent and utterly over-riding authority of the religious claim upon us?

Yes, there is one way – by internalizing the religious claim as an
a priori practical principle. The crucial insight is that metaphysical
facts can no more make religious values binding than they can
make moral values binding. The religious claim upon us therefore
has to be autonomous, in a way for which the best philosophical
model and precedent is Kant's treatment of morality. The religious
precedent is the way the Buddha put spirituality above theology
by exalting the Dharma above the Gods. The Way comes first. Get
the Way right, and talk of the Gods can be allowed to make its
own kind of sense as best it can. In addition, I believe Kierkegaard
in many of his writings was fairly close to the position here described. He seems to dismiss the cosmological and objective side
of religion, locates God at the centre of an intensified human
subjectivity, and speaks of 'the Eternal' somewhat as I speak of
'the religious requirement'.[2]

At any rate, the argument leads us to a position that can be
summarized as follows:

(*i*) It seems doubtful whether there is any immense cosmic or
supracosmic Creator-Mind. Even if there is, it is hard to see what
it or he could have to do with religion. But nowadays nobody is
likely to postulate the existence of such a being for any but religious

reasons. Remove that religious interest in the issue, and there is nothing left of it.

(*ii*) Objective theism therefore does not matter so much as people think. What matters is spirituality; and a modern spirituality must be a spirituality for a fully-unified autonomous human consciousness, for that is the kind of consciousness that modern people have. This in turn means that the principles of spirituality cannot be imposed upon us from without and cannot depend at all upon any external circumstances. On the contrary, the principles of spirituality must be fully internalized *a priori* principles, freely adopted and self-imposed. A modern person must not any more surrender the apex of his self-consciousness to a god. It must remain his own.

(*iii*) The highest and central principle of spirituality (the religious requirement, as it is often called below) is the one that commands us to become spirit, that is, precisely to attain the highest degree of autonomous self-knowledge and self-transcendence. To achieve this we must escape from 'craving' or 'carnal lusts' and the false ego thereby created, and we must seek perfect purity of heart, disinterestedness, quiet and recollected alertness and so on. The subsidiary principles of spirituality are therefore conditions for attaining the goal to which the central principle directs us.

(*iv*) What then is God? God is a unifying symbol that eloquently personifies and represents to us everything that spirituality requires of us. The requirement is the will of God, the divine attributes represent to us various aspects of the spiritual life, and God's nature as spirit represents the goal we are to attain. Thus the whole of the spiritual life revolves around God and is summed up in God. God is the religious concern, reified.

It is possible to have a non-theistic spirituality, as in Buddhism, but on our account the gap between it and theism is largely closed. For the job which in our view is done by God is on the Buddhist view distributed between the Dharma and Nirvana. God both represents to us what we are to become and shows us the way to become it; union with God is the goal and the love of God is the way.

(*v*) Is there any extra-religious and objective existence of God? There is a paradox here, for there cannot and must not be any religious interest in any extra-religious existence of God; such a thing would be a frivolous distraction. Yet on the other hand many will complain that a God who has no describable reality except the reality that he has in relation to human religiousness is too 'subjective'. One ought not to make too many concessions to this latter point of view, for unless religiousness is truly autonomous and subjective it is not religiously commendable. I say again: piety cannot in any way be validated from outside. Religious activity must be purely disinterested and therefore cannot depend upon any external facts such as an objective God or a life after death. Furthermore, spiritual autonomy must not on any account be prejudiced, because there is no salvation without it. So it is spiritual vulgarity and immaturity to demand an extra-religious reality of God.

Nevertheless, the spiritual life is teleologically ordered. It is goal-seeking, oriented towards a *focus imaginarius*. The Buddhists have what is still probably the best representation of this goal in their concept of Nirvana. Like Nirvana, God may be thought of as transcendent but unspecifiable, an ideal focus of aspiration that does not come so far forward into either objectivity or determinacy as to prejudice the quest for disinterestedness. But this concession is intended to be minimal. Ordinarily one ought to live *etsi deus non daretur* (as if God were not given), at any rate so far as any objective deity is concerned.

(*vi*) It is spiritually important that one should not believe in life after death but should instead strive to attain the goal of the spiritual life in history. It is in this life, and in relation to social and economic conditions objectively and presently prevailing, that we have to struggle to realize religious values.

At this point we diverge sharply from Hegel, whose doctrine of Spirit or *Geist* was intended to synthesize the demands of individual freedom and social obligation. *Geist* seeks the realization of the individual as autonomous and rational spiritual subject, for *Geist* itself comes to its own fulfilment precisely in and only in such individuals. But *Geist* is also active on the world-historical plane, for Hegel thought that in his time the whole world-historical movement favoured the development of autonomous individual spirituality as he conceived it. Hence there was no conflict between the claims of individual spirituality and the claims of public life as a citizen of the ethical state. The two sets of claims exactly coincided and to fulfil the one was to fulfil the other also.

We cannot be so optimistic as Hegel about either nature or society. Our natural science presents us with a mechanistic and disenchanted view of nature and the modern state, whether in its socialist or its capitalist form, is utilitarian, bureaucratic and the uncomprehending enemy of spirit. Furthermore, the relationship between human activities and the world of nature is well known to be incipiently disastrous with no prospect of getting into balance. Hence the modern spiritual individual cannot be in a harmonious relationship to modern society. He cannot help but be in some measure inwardly alienated, for he lives by another value scale. He is a critic and protester who has here no continuing city. Hegel thought there was something deeply wrong and unsatisfactory about such a relation to the world and he may be right from the metaphysical point of view, but he is wholly wrong from the religious point of view. From the religious point of view such a relationship to the world (characteristic of Christianity from its beginning in the message of Jesus) is highly advantageous, for it intensifies inwardness and accelerates spiritual development. We sometimes wonder how Aristotle's magnanimous public man could also have known how to practise the contemplative life and its virtues, and Hegel's synthesis raises the same question. If one is as harmoniously conformed to the world as Hegel's citizen, how can one have any real inwardness or spirituality at all? On the view I propose, the Christian, the world is evil and one can only be delivered from the world by principles of spirituality which are not of the world, but which inescapably and rightly set one to some extent at odds with the world. It seems strange to say that our highest good can be had only by appropriating principles that as it were put one at an angle to life, but it is so. For our highest good is to become spirit and we must do it in this life, for there is no other so far as we can tell. To become spirit we must transcend nature, and to do that we need to adopt a supernatural requirement which can lever us free from the world. For the law is, the more you lose the more you gain; the more you are free from the world, the richer you become.

Such, in brief, is the point of view here defended. No doubt it is not entirely novel. That spirituality precedes doctrine, that the correspondence theory of truth is a poor tool to use for assessing religious beliefs, that on the contrary much of religious language and ritual is expressive rather than descriptive in its force, and that theological realism is therefore a crude mistake – all this has been said often enough before. Add to it that many modern people wish to preserve something of religious spirituality, values and attitudes in an epoch when human consciousness is no longer even residually heteronomous, and our thesis begins to take shape. The argument that follows will attempt to exhibit it as a permissible and appropriate transformation of the received religious tradition.

Can this be done? I think it must. Commentators on religious affairs, bemoaning the enfeebled spiritual condition of modern religion, sometimes betray a quite unrealistic and sentimental expectation that modern religious people, if sincere, should have an archaic form of consciousness. Of course they do not. I have met a fair sprinkling of patriarchs, cardinals, bishops, monks and other prominent religious persons and can assure the world that they all have the modern form of consciousness and that not a single one of them believes in God in quite the pre-modern way. It would indeed be unhistorical to expect otherwise. So if twentieth-century churchmen have a fully twentieth-century form of consciousness, some account needs to be given of how it is possible for one with such a consciousness to be sincerely religious in a Christian way. Unfortunately what we find in practice is that most people do not address themselves to this all-important question. The great majority of religious intellectuals nowadays take an extremely depressing line which I can only call conservative scepticism. On questions of meaning they profess themselves strong theological realists and they declare their unshakable allegiance to a vanished world in which the prevailing cultural conditions made it possible really to believe in objective theism. We do not have that particular mode of consciousness any longer because we do not live in that world any more, but (say they) let us hang on, let us hope the tide will turn, and in the meantime we will continue to believe even if it has to be belief at one remove. We have not and cannot have an authentic living faith ourselves, but at least we can stand in solidarity with those in former days for whom an authentic top-drawer living faith was a live option, lucky devils.

Unfortunately it is their attachment to theological realism which prevents such people from reaching a first-hand modern religiousness. For theological realism can only actually be *true* for a heteronomous consciousness such as no normal person ought now to have. So if the theological realists are right then Christianity has indeed to be spoken of in the past tense and can only be believed at one remove, which in effect means that it must be believed aesthetically and not religiously. Aesthetic admiration for the religious past replaces living religion.

How can I, without intellectual prestidigitation, weaken the grip of theological realism on your mind? I cannot realistically claim that the traditional men of faith from Moses to Wesley were after all not realists, so do not imagine that I am going so far as that. All I am claiming is that the tradition is not rigidly and uniformly realist. There are some elements within it that can be singled out, built on and developed along non-realist lines. But I am out to change the tradition and not to claim that it was other than it was.

There will certainly be suspicion about my style of argument, for Anglo-Saxon philosophy is anti-historical and reluctant to admit that all intellectual traditions are maintained by the kind of reinterpretation and transposition that I am here doing. I can only beg to be given a hearing and say that it is not only the tradition that I am transposing but also my own convictions hitherto. For over the years I have tried to combine belief in God with spiritual freedom by pressing the themes of the 'negative theology' and the divine transcendence ever harder. Eventually I was saying that God does not determine and cannot be thought of as determining the spiritual life from outside, for God is altogether unspecifiable. God had to become objectively thinner and thinner in order to allow subjective religiousness to expand. It is only one step further to the objectively atheous position here propounded. But my God is still the *deus absconditus*, the hidden God who is found at last to hide himself in the depths of the heart. He never was and is not now the *deus otiosus*, the redundant God like the Greek sky-god Ouranos whose functions became so general and so exalted that he disappeared, promoted into obscurity.

I have had no choice but to be rather painfully explicit. A number of previous theologies that have been moving in the same direction as this have suffered badly by trying to claim too much in the way of continuity with the preceding tradition. In order not to offend the traditionalists, the theologian conceals the full extent of his own radicalism and tries to appear more orthodox than he really is. This makes his language ambiguous, for what he says seems designed to mean one thing to the faithful and something else to the outsider, and people begin to suspect him of being a typical apologist – a confidence-trickster. His assumption of an appearance of modernity is not sincere but merely tactical. Under the attractive bait is hidden the same cruel old trap.

Alternatively, if the radical theologian be given the benefit of the doubt and assumed to be sincere in what he says the position is even worse. Evidently he suffers from a defect of consciousness, he himself failing to realize the inner meaning and drift of his own language. This is fatal, for nowadays no religious message can be true unless through it one can attain a higher degree of consciousness than one's non-religious contemporaries. Religion has to give one wit, levity and command; religion that makes the believer dull, benighted and obtuse is not spiritual and has to be rejected. So one must not purchase a specious doctrinal respectability at the price of loss of lucidity and therefore religious failure.

Explicitness then it has to be, for true religion is spiritual limpidity. And, putting it plainly, modern consciousness is now almost completely autonomous. This is a marvellous thing, but even if you regret it there is still no possibility of reverting to heteronomy. So we cannot (and ought not to) believe in an objective deity who among other things antecedently prescribes our moral values and our spiritual itinerary from outside.

However, the autonomous consciousness still needs religion as much as ever. In particular it needs a spirituality to give it shape and make it productive. Such a spirituality cannot be inferred from any supposed external metaphysical facts. It must take the form of a set of freely chosen and self-imposed *a priori* principles. We must choose our own religious values because they are intrinsically precious, rather than because any external being commands us to adopt them and threatens us with sanctions. There are reasons for thinking that the best set of such values is the Christian set.

And what is God? The Christian doctrine of God just is Christian spirituality in coded form, for God is a symbol that represents to us everything that spirituality requires of us and promises to us.

2

THE DECLINE OF OBJECTIVE THEISM

The Great Defection

Most plain men – and plain philosophers too, for that matter – take a realist view of God. That is, they think the position is that either God exists or God does not exist, because God at least purports to be an actually-existing independent individual being. Admittedly it must be allowed that God is a special case, for he is also held to be a world-transcending infinite Spirit, unlimited and illimitable in power, wisdom and goodness. If he exists it cannot be in just the same way that you and I exist for, unlike other things that we think of as really existing, God cannot be located in the great field of cause-and-effect interactions that is the world. God is active everywhere in the world, people say, and yet he is not part of it and cannot be pointed out within it. Furthermore God's existence also differs from ours in that whereas we exist only for a short time, God always exists and cannot cease to be or be threatened in any way. If there was ever a God there is always a God, and there cannot ever not be a God.

From all this it is clear that God is a special case, and if we say God exists we say it in a stretched or extended sense appropriate to God's unique case. All the same, those plain men and plain philosophers insist, whether or not there is a God remains at bottom a factual question. We may approach an empty-looking house, call into it, and find out either that it is occupied or that it is not; and similarly one who cries out in prayer either talks to someone who is there or fails to talk to anyone. Theists and atheists disagree, in the end, about what there is. Theists say that someone hears when we pray, and atheists say there is nobody listening.

Such is the realistic view of God that nearly everyone begins with and most people stick to, whether they are believers or not. It is wrong and I am going to show how and why it is wrong; but it is the common view and we are bound to start from it. Its clarity and crudity give it some advantages, and in particular it brings out very sharply the magnitude of the huge historical process that we call the decline of religion in the modern world.

For suppose first that God does exist. Then what an awesome and almost apocalyptic event is the great defection from God that has gathered pace over the past two centuries or so! If God does exist in the way the realists suppose him to, then it is imperative to produce some sort of theological theory of the decline of religion and the apparent eclipse of God in modern times. How can God have permitted it to occur?

Alternatively, suppose atheist humanism is correct and that God does not exist. Then how are we to explain the extraordinary fact that (with only a few exceptions) the whole human race up to the late seventeenth century laboured in bondage to a religious view of the world? Can a humanist or rationalist give an adequate explanation of the rise and maintenance of an illusion so colossal, so ancient and so widespread? All credit to those individuals who have seen the need to produce an error-theory adequate to the facts – Feuerbach, Marx, Durkheim, Freud and (most recently) Julian Jaynes.[1]

It is not surprising that so many modern thinkers have been preoccupied with the remarkable gulf between modern secular scientific-industrial culture and all other societies. Ernest Gellner, who has written shrewdly about it, boldly describes all cultures other than our own as 'non-epistemic'.[2] By our standards they were almost without knowledge. It is not just that they had less than a thousandth of the information available to us, nor just that their trial-and-error crafts and skills were unsupported by a vast body of powerful theoretical knowledge, nor even that before the seventeenth century there were scarcely any laws of nature expressed in mathematical form. It is rather that cultures other than our own entirely lacked properly established procedures – and professionals – to criticize existing knowledge and generate, test, organize and apply new knowledge. By our standards it is something of a marvel that they managed to survive at all. On the other hand, by their standards we are shiftless, faithless, chaotic, corrupt and doomed. It is easy for us to forget with what moral repugnance Western society is often regarded by the more backward countries

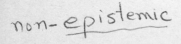

non-epistemic

of the Third World and the socialistic bloc. That judgment is a
mistake, but it is an understandable mistake. It is a mistake that
reflects the huge gap between traditional and modern societies —
and, by the way, the socialist countries, being closed, ideological,
tightly-disciplined and conservative, in many ways resemble traditional societies more than modern, which is why they seem in
many cases to be so successful in preserving traditional religion!

From Tradition to Modernity

For some societies the modern world arrived in ships on a particular day, but the transition from traditional to modern culture is
not always so tidy as that. In Europe we have long regarded
classical antiquity as in many respects foreshadowing the modern
world in its pluralism, its tradition of secular science and philosophy, and the naturalism and scepticism of some of its traditions
of thought. At the other extreme, pockets of peasant life still remain
in modern Europe. The changeover from traditional to modern
culture has not been clearcut, and no doubt some would deny that
it has even occurred or ever will occur. Ever since the rise of Greek
philosophy the two ways of thinking have coexisted and struggled
with each other and — according to this account — human thought
is never likely to become either wholly mythological-traditional or
wholly technological-utilitarian. There will always be some kind of
mix of the two mentalities.

So say those who are reluctant to admit that a radical and
permanent change in the human condition has taken place. The
best way to answer them is to sketch out what is meant by the
change from tradition to modernity. It can be summarized under
four headings.

First, in *cosmology* it is a changeover from the old sacred, highly-
wrought, finite cosmos to the new 'meaningless', boundless mechanical universe. In the old cosmology the universe was very
complex and populous. It was like a very rich literary text, full of
hidden symbolism. Values, purposes, omens, portents, occult forces
and meanings abounded in everything. A human being's proper
fulfilment lay in harmoniously fitting himself into this vast given
order of meanings and values, and the principle held not merely at
the individual level but also at the social, for the social order was
thought to mirror the cosmic order.

By contrast, we have experienced the disenchantment of the
world. For us the world is what the sciences of nature have shown

it to be – morally and religiously neutral and without magic. It is
bureaucratic, in the sense that all particular events are processed
in accordance with general rules, and this regularity and law-abidingness is for us the only point of correspondence between the
social order and the natural. In order to learn to see what nature
is really like we have been obliged quite consciously to forego all
the old rich 'meaningfulness'. The process has not been entirely
one of loss. The lion and the fox may not be quite what they were
in the old iconographies, bestiaries, fables and nursery tales, but
we have discovered their real private lives to be nevertheless genuinely interesting in their own right. The new scientific view of
nature is by no means impoverished in the sense of being either
banal or lacking in complexity. What has happened is rather that
we have come to separate the territories of science, art, morality
and religion whereas formerly they were all fused together in the
way people saw the world.

Secondly, with the change in cosmology comes a corresponding
change in the nature of *knowledge*. In the old order 'knowledge'
meant pre-eminently a fixed body of sacred traditional material
which it was vital to keep intact, and the communion with the
divine that was to be had through it. The mind does not autonomously generate new knowledge, but obediently conforms itself
to a perfect body of saving truth that is presented to it by God and
tradition. This view of sacred knowledge also affected men's attitude to their knowledge of nature. It too was seen as a sort of
sacred text, charged with divine meaning. Knowledge of the world
was by participation; the mind accommodated itself to an objective
order of intelligible essences.

Modern knowledge is quite different. It is man-made, critically-
established, unmysterious, ever-expanding and subject to continual
revision. In many respects it is very strong – its sheer quantity, its
power of self-criticism and very rapid growth, and the unpre-
cedented technical power that it has brought. Unfortunately there
is another kind of strength that it lacks, and that is the distinctive
kind of strength that the old religious knowledge did have. Divine
knowledge of the sort they had in pre-modern societies gave intense
religious happiness, spiritual fortitude and stability of a kind we
have now lost.

Thirdly, the disconnection of society from the cosmic order and
from the constraint of tradition drastically affects the way people
think about all the leading *social institutions*. In traditional society
these institutions – language, the family, the moral and social

order, ritual, kingship and so on – are thought of as divinely
ordained. But in modern society they come to be thought of as all
of them products of history, man-made and subject to continuous
development and modification in order to keep pace with social
change. An amusing and late example of the old way of thinking
is Robert Filmer's *Patriarcha* of 1680, which deduces the divine
right of kings from the sovereignty that God gave to Adam over
his family and over the whole created order. But Filmer was at the
end of the line. At the time when he wrote his style of argument
was already an anachronism, for the English revolution had occurred and Locke was about to issue his *Treatises on Civil Government* and his *Letters concerning Toleration*. The state was
beginning to be seen more on the analogy of a voluntary association
whose rules have to be agreed by its members and which gains its
authority from their consent. When social institutions come thus
to be seen as man-made, and therefore full of human imperfection
and always needing reform, there is a price to be paid. Restlessness,
social tensions and chronic discontent become in some degree legitimate and even desirable, because they are the dynamo of social
change and progress.

(4) Fourthly and finally, the *self* changes in the movement from
tradition to modernity. The traditional individual found his own
nature, situation in life and destiny all readymade for him. Guided
by providence, he followed a predestined path through life. By
contrast, the modern person is no longer content to live his life so
completely within an antecedently-prescribed framework. He
wants to define himself, to posit and pursue his own goals and to
choose for himself what to make of himself. A classic example of
the revolt against tradition is the rebellion of young Asians in
modern Britain against arranged marriages and against the constraints of family and culture.

  In connection with this a point needs to be made about the
affirmation, repeatedly heard since the Enlightenment, that man
has now come of age. It is often objected to this that on the
contrary modern man is making grotesquely poor use of his vaunt-
ed freedom. This objection entirely misses the moral point, which
is about autonomy and not about happiness or competence or
moral success or maturity. We can well imagine one of those Asians
saying, 'I would rather make my own sort of a mess of my own
life than have somebody else make his kind of success of my life
for me!' The issue is *autonomy*, and once one has understood the
possibility of autonomy for oneself then one is under a moral

necessity to seize it and on no account ever to renounce it voluntarily.

Such are some of the main features of the changeover from traditional to modern culture. In European terms the ideas I have just sketched first became commonplace during the Enlightenment. It is clear that they present a severe challenge to traditional religious belief, but the precise nature of the challenge is not always noticed. The point is that objective monotheism is the crowning intellectual achievement of traditional culture, both synthesizing and ratifying all its typical concerns. The God of objective monotheism is traditional culture personified. He unifies its values and symbolizes its authority. I need not spell this out in relation to the divine creation of social institutions and the natural order; let us instead merely note one or two other aspects of divine authority in traditional society.

Monotheism strongly endorses the traditional ideal of knowledge, for knowledge is the conformation of the mind to intelligible reality, and God is both supreme intelligence and intelligible supreme reality. Divinity is therefore the supreme and in the end almost the only knowledge.

Again, traditional culture merges the world of fact and the world of value, and so does theism. God is supreme in the order of being and in the order of value, his will decreeing in a single eternal act both what is the case and what ought to be the case. Both are one, for God is one. In him fact and value must ultimately coincide.

Furthermore, in God the absolute fullness of knowledge and goodness are eternally actual. It is not for man to seek to invent his own forms of knowledge and goodness for himself, but rather through prayer and obedience to seek them from God. Thus to an objective monotheist the notion of man's autonomous creation of knowledge and of the moral order must appear abhorrent and indeed as treason against God.

Lastly, God is all-powerful, all-wise, all-good and the All-Determiner who prescribes our entire lives for us. Must it not be, then, that the community with the most exalted theology of the divine sovereignty – Islam – will also be the one which is the most heteronomous and most rigidly traditionalist? Conversely, as man gains in autonomy God must presumably retire from objectivity.

In these and other ways it would appear that the traditional realist understanding of God belongs entirely to traditional culture and must vanish with the changeover to the modern outlook. At the very least, a considerable revision of belief in God seems to be

required. Certainly the problem of God's relation to human autonomy preoccupied the series of great thinkers who revived speculative philosophy towards the end of the age of Enlightenment –
Kant, Fichte, Hegel and others.[3]

The Proofs Break Down

In view of all this it is not surprising that people have lost confidence in the traditional proofs of God's existence. By now, indeed,
we are used to hearing religious believers freely acknowledge that
of course the existence of God cannot be proved. But can one
admit this and still continue to hold a realist belief in God?

The old theistic proofs have turned out over the centuries to be
very elastic. They can be and have been restated in an endless
variety of new ways, and in any case hardly anything in philosophy
has ever been conclusively proved or disproved without any dis-
senting voice. So it is not to be expected that there should be
unanimous agreement about either the formulation or the criticism
of the proofs. All I need to produce, for the purpose of the present
argument, is sufficient reason for doubting whether any of the
proofs can be made secure against attack while still accomplishing
something significant in support of a realist account of God.

The most interesting and remarkable of the traditional proofs is
the 'ontological argument' – a misnomer, but the name has Kant's
authority – which was classically formulated by Anselm of Can-
terbury. Anselm drew upon hints in the platonic tradition and
particularly in Augustine, and his argument still attracts philosophers because it is a test case: can pure philosophical reasoning
by itself establish major facts about the nature of reality? Idealist
philosophers want to answer yes, and so they keep reviving the
argument in new forms; though in view of what I have already
said about human autonomy in the modern period it is not surprising that these idealists have tended to describe God as immanent within the movement of autonomous human reason, and to
see the ontological argument as epitomizing the unfolding of reality
in and through the self-unfolding of reason. All of which is rather
different from Anselm's original concern.

Put at its simplest, Anselm's argument begins by pointing out
that for the believer God would not be God if he could be surpassed
in any way. God is not just the greatest actual being but the greatest
conceivable being. Now does such a being exist in reality, or is he
merely ideal? He must exist in reality, for to exist in reality is

tautology —

greater than to be a mere idea. A God who existed only in thought would be surpassed in greatness by an actual God, which (God being by definition unsurpassable) is absurd. So if God is truly unsurpassable – which he is, by definition – then he must be real.

This argument uses a *reductio ad absurdum*, so let us use one against it in turn and prove by the same method the existence of a loudest possible noise. Is the loudest possible noise actual, or merely ideal? It must be actual, for actual noises are after all much louder than merely imagined ones. A loudest possible noise that existed only in thought would be surpassed in loudness by any actual loud noise, which is absurd. So the loudest possible noise must exist in reality.

What is the fallacy? The word 'loudest' suggests comparison on a continuous scale in respect of a certain quality. But for the argument to work a different kind of comparison had also to be built into the concept 'loudest' from the outset, namely the comparison between something that is merely thought and the same thing actually existing. But if the superior loudness of actual noises over thought ones is in this way built in from the start, the argument must be a mere tautology. It cannot be doing any more than unpacking the initial definition of 'loudest'.

Similarly, in the case of the greatest-being argument, the word 'greatest' suggests that God is being thought of as unsurpassable in his possession of various perfections – none can be wiser than God and none more good. But for the argument to work, the term 'greatest' must also have had built into it all along the rather different idea that for something to exist in reality is 'greater' than for just the same thing to be merely an object of thought. God, it turns out, was from the start defined in such a way that it can be deduced from his definition that he exists. A definition has been analysed, but nothing new has been proved. The argument may have shown that God is *thought of by believers* as 'necessarily' existing, but the argument has not shown that God does in fact exist.

May it be that the argument, though admittedly invalid in all other applications, is nonetheless valid in respect of God because in this case alone the supreme all-round perfection of the object thought guarantees its existence, God's existence being one of his perfections? I doubt if this makes sense; for consider two concepts of a certain object, say a glass marble. Concept A has the content *round, hard, clear* and concept B has the content *round, hard, clear* and *existing*. Now there cannot be any difference between the range of objects A applies to and the range of objects B applies to.[4] Existence, built into a concept, makes no difference whatever to the range of that concept's real application. And surely it is as true of God as of any other object that whether his concept applies to anything is not itself part of the concept. So what meaning can there be in calling existence a quality or perfection? 'Ah', it is replied, 'Existence may not be a perfection, but *necessary* existence is.' Does that make sense? I do not think so. There is an appeal here to the old platonic idea of degrees of being. Physical objects are things of which it makes sense to say that they might not have existed, whereas there is no sense in saying that numbers might not have existed; so that numbers, it is claimed, are things more real and perfect and enduring than physical objects. Now I can see no sense in constructing such a scale of degrees of reality, for what can be the meaning of saying that purely abstract entities like numbers are 'more real' than physical ones like cats? Still more, what can be the use of projecting the scale further and claiming that as a number is more real than a cat, so God is more real than a number, having the maximal conceivable degree of whatever it is that this 'reality' or 'perfection' is supposed to be? All this makes no sense at all, yet the ontological argument cannot help but involve us in such absurdities, for it claims to be a proof of the God of religion from premises that are true *a priori*, like the principles of logic and mathematics. Yet if this is really so, then its conclusion must be an *a priori* truth also, and God must be an entity of approximately the same kind as a mathematical or logical object; and that is surely not compatible with theological realism, which usually describes God as personal, loving and intelligent. Realists do not believe in a God who is as abstract as a number. Altogether, it seems unlikely that the ontological argument can be formulated in a way that is valid and proves something of interest; and it also seems that even if it can be so formulated it will not help the cause of theological realism. The argument can be linked with a realist view of God only via platonic metaphysics, which takes a realist view of abstract entities. Take it out of that context, and it does not imply a realist view of God at all. On the contrary, it suggests that God is just ideal.

Anselm's argument makes no reference to the world of creatures. It belongs in a context of monastic spirituality and the study of Augustine. *Noverim me, noverim te:*[5] it is evident to Augustine and Anselm that there is one and only one supreme concern of the human mind, namely God. By contrast, the various trains of reasoning that are grouped under the label 'the cosmological argument' move from the world to God and seek to place God in relation to the world. Since they attempt to relate the divine existence to that of creatures they seem to be closer to the concern of the theological realist. By comparing and contrasting the being of God with the being of creatures such arguments should help to make clear what it is to speak of God's reality.

What then might be the basis for an argument from the world to God? Since Thomas Aquinas set out his Five Ways there have been three main kinds of answer.

As Thomas himself saw it, there are within the world of experience certain relations between things which are irreflexive and transitive. Thomas has in mind the following principal examples:

. . . is moved by . . .

. . . is efficiently caused by . . .

. . . is dependent upon . . .

. . is inferior in worth to . . .

. . . is guided and directed by . . .

Each of these five types of relation generates a series, and the series cannot be endless because (so Thomas had been led by Aristotle to suppose) there is something repugnant to reason in the idea of an actual infinite series. But there is a further point: Thomas' conception of the universe was profoundly hierarchical. Every one of the five relations was for him a relation between a lesser and a greater in which the greater communicates 'reality' to the lesser. So as one moves up the series one mounts up a ladder of degrees of reality towards the Most Real Being of all. One ascends from finite beings down here on earth to the elements, the heavenly bodies, the angels and so, ultimately and inevitably, to God.

In Thomas' view then, the mere existence of one or more of these five types of relation among creatures is enough to show that the world cannot be a closed and autonomous cyclical system. On the contrary, the world is activated from outside, and not just from outside, but from above – that is, by a being of greater reality. This supreme being must be Prime Mover, First Cause, and an absolutely independent Being of supreme worth who governs all things and is the dynamo of the whole universe.

Such were Thomas' own opinions, and they were utterly destroyed by the scientific revolution of the seventeenth century which simply abandoned his ideas of motion, causality and so forth and began to represent the workings of nature as autonomous. It has continued to do so with increasing success ever since, and none of Thomas' arguments can possibly be defended now in quite the form in which he first advanced it.

Layers of reinterpretation have therefore come to be superimposed upon Thomas, and the second type of argument from the world to God is the argument from contingency that is based upon the third of his Five Ways.

It is claimed that creatures are profoundly unstable. They are all contingent. They could have been otherwise, and there is no contradiction in supposing that they might not have existed at all. Indeed the whole world, and every detail of it, is a might-not-have-been. Why is there anything at all, and why this world and not some other?

As the exposition proceeds it becomes apparent that two slightly different arguments are being put forward, one to the effect that the world is ontologically insufficient, and the other saying that an ultimate explanation is needed. Taking first the claim that the world and everything in it is contingent in the sense of being ontologically insufficient, Thomas himself seems to have thought that the action of a necessary being is needed to bring a contingent thing into existence, and that the whole world of contingent things needs continuous propping-up and support from outside. But I do not know what he means. What is unsatisfying about the fact that the sentences in which I describe a particular state of affairs in the real world are not necessary truths? They cannot be so. Necessary truths are universal, whereas I am describing just one particular state of affairs. A description of just one state of affairs obviously cannot be a universal truth. And what can it mean to say that the world is weak, unstable, and in need of a creator's support? Things do not just vanish, matter and energy are (with some qualifications) conserved, and the way the world behaves is to a large extent explicable and predictable. Contrary to what is sometimes suggested, the world's submicroscopic structure is beautifully regular. What more is there that might be the case and ought to be the case but is not the case? Are Thomas and his followers saying that they will only be fully satisfied if the world-process unfolds by pure rational necessity, so that the existence and nature of everything can be deduced from its concept? I suspect that that is indeed what they are saying. If the world of fact is disparagingly called merely contingent, there must be lurking in the background the contrasting idea of a better world that is really solid and intellectually-satisfactory because it all unfolds by rational necessity. If the world were like that we would have no cause for complaint, for it would be luminously evident why every thing is and is just as it is.

But this is to revive the fallacy of the ontological argument, that something can be constrained into existence by logical necessity. And in any case it is not quite the conclusion that St Thomas and his followers are trying to reach. What they are saying is that the world is merely contingent and in need of support and explanation from outside, and their problem is to give this remarkable claim a meaning. They do it by saying that the world might, just might, have been logically necessary and therefore in no need of any external propping-up; but since the world is not logically necessary, it evidently does need support. However, there is no meaning in their suggestion that the world might have been logically necessary and in no need of explanation. So they have not managed to describe another way the world might have been, by contrast with which it can appear meaningful to say that this world is contingent and does need an external support and explanation. Thus it appears that arguments of this type from the world to God are invalid. No meaning has been given to the claim that the world is in need of external support.

But now we have come to the third variant of the cosmological proof, the one that says the world needs a transcendent explanation. Again there is a peculiar ambiguity. In religious language from the Bible onwards, talk of God is commonly offered, not as an explanation, but as a way of reconciling oneself to the inexplicable. God's will and ways are inscrutable. When we complain that something dire has happened and are told to 'See it as God's will', we are being advised to keep quiet, to stop complaining, to have faith and to endure. It is obvious that since we know much less of how God works than we do of how the world works, the appeal to God explains nothing at all. The appeal to God tells us nothing, but nothing, of why one person dies young and another lives to a green old age, or why one person has faith and another despairs. It is not suggested that the world proceeds necessarily from God, nor that we can explain why God designed things just this way and not otherwise; so in what sense is God postulated as the 'explanation' of the world?[6]

At this point a somewhat different way of thinking about God is introduced. It was first and best formulated by the philosopher Leibniz. Instead of stressing the inscrutability of God's will, it sees God's will as determined by his perfectly good and rational nature. The claim is that, by the principle of sufficient reason, there must be an ultimate explanation of the universe. Such an ultimate explanation will exhibit the universe as the product of a rational choice of the best by a being unlimited in knowledge and power. Hence God exists and this is the best of all possible worlds.

But an argument of this kind can only work on two conditions; first the applicability of the principle of sufficient reason to the Universe as a whole must be shown (which is itself a tough enough task), and secondly the philosopher must actually show that this is the best of all possible worlds. He must solve the problem of evil. This Leibniz failed to do. He attempted to show *a priori* and in very general terms that God must have reviewed the alternatives and have decided that this would be the best of all possible worlds, but he did not even attempt to show in detail how it actually is so.

For consider some particular frightful, futile and disastrous evil. There are many philosophical theologians still willing to claim along traditional lines that God's good providence directs all the world-process, in a 'realistic' sense. And they will claim that this particular frightful evil need not necessarily refute that belief in providence. But that means they are able to make only a negative claim: 'If you have good antecedent reasons, on other grounds, for believing in providence (understood, again, in a realistic sense) then that belief might just be able to survive confrontation with the facts of evil.'

What nobody claims, or can claim, is to be able to show positively that such evils are rationally appropriate expressions of the divine goodness and wisdom. Nobody in his right mind thinks he can actually demonstrate that the holocaust of European Jewry was a fitting expression of the divine providence. And therefore a Leibnizian proof of God as the ultimate explanation of the world has not been delivered. We are not actually given the sufficient reason for the holocaust; we are told that there must be a reason and a God who knows it, but as to what it *is* we are none the wiser. Although it is often claimed that a realistic belief in God provides the most intellectually-satisfying ultimate explanation of life, the sense in which the explanation is actually provided for us is very tenuous. What it seems to amount to is this: it is alleged to be intellectually unsatisfying that the world should be plural, contingent and changing. The mind seeks some unifying principle behind the facade of plurality and change. That unifying principle is the 'explanation'. But why should it be the God of monotheism? There are many other possible candidates, such as those explored in Indian religious philosophy, and it seems that they cannot be excluded, for theists themselves say creation is voluntary and it is not possible to deduce the detail of the world from the divine nature. But this is to admit that the way the world hangs together in God's mind remains quite unknown, and no real explaining has been done.

Many of the same limitations trouble the argument from design, which of all the traditional proofs seems to imply the most realistic view of God, and is the most open to the charges of inflated explanatory pretensions and vulnerability to the challenge of evil.

By 'inflated explanatory pretensions' I mean simply that the design argument does not do nearly as much explaining as its proponents have claimed; indeed, when we compare it with Darwin's ways of explaining the structure and behaviour of organisms we soon realize that it does almost no real explaining at all. Because Darwin's principles of explanation are immanent, functional and 'historical' they really illuminate the mutual adaptation of insect and orchid, the stag's antlers and the peacock's courtship. By contrast William Paley's view of nature, based on the argument from design, is strangely uninformative. Paley claims that there is a benevolent world-making and world-directing providence. Can we then specify what the purpose of cosmic history is and predict the next few turns in the plot? – Of course not. Can we at least say for sure that nothing very nasty is going to happen to us? – No. Here is an attractive, edible-looking red berry on a plant that I have never seen before: can I safely predict from the theory of the Great Designer's benevolence that this berry will turn out to be nutritious? – I certainly cannot. Then just how informative is Paley's theory?

These questions illustrate a curious and significant fact about theological realism, namely the ease with which under interrogation it collapses into its opposite. Of all the many forms that belief in God can take the design argument seems to be the most literal or realistic in its assumptions. It proposes God as an empirical hypothesis to account for the facts of the world's structure and workings. It is as naively literal and anthropomorphic as can be, representing theological statements as being of the same kind as scientific statements.

But it is punished for having been so straightforward, by being interrogated as if it were indeed the plain empirical hypothesis that it pretends to be. Under questioning it is exposed as having no explanatory or predictive value to speak of. Then can it at least be falsified? No, apparently not, because sufficiently ingenious apologists can continue indefinitely to meet objections drawn from the facts of evil and disharmony in the world by extending the free will defence. However horrific and all-encompassing the facts of evil, they never quite seem able to refute the realist view of God's good providence. Thus we arrive at an *impasse*. The empirical theist put all his money on the claim that the ideas of God's design and providential government of the world are factual in the sort of way that scientific knowledge is factual. Yet it now turns out that they fail to satisfy the standard criteria of a scientific hypothesis. If they turn out not to be factual in the way that they themselves claim to be, it seems reasonable to conclude that they are not factual at all. Thus we feel forced to a purely attitudinal or subjective view of belief in God. To say, 'God's in his heaven!' is merely another way of saying, 'All's right with the world!' Both expressions are simply optimistic exclamations.

So much for the three best known arguments for the existence of God, and their relation to theological realism. Three other ways to God deserve a brief mention. They appeal respectively to religious experience, to the foundations of knowledge, and to morality. Yet in each case, I suggest, the argument is not particularly friendly to the realist view of God.

Put at its simplest, the argument from religious experience states that we may be sure that God exists because many people enjoy direct experience of God.

The claim being made here is very strange, for what worldly experience could there be which could justify us in making a distinction between the whole world of experience and something which transcends it? Is this notion coherent? However, let us suppose that it is. Perhaps there is a God who transcends the world and has created a special way in which some fortunate people can have experience of him. What could this special way be?

At this point philosophers traditionally consider the suggestion that religious experience is acquired by an extra sense which some people have and others lack. This theory has seemed appropriate because a sighted man, for example, gains genuine information about his environment in a way that is beyond the understanding of a congenitally blind man. Similarly, it is suggested that the mystic may be able to gain genuine knowledge in a way beyond the rest of us because he has some special sense organ or faculty that we lack.

There might be something in this analogy if mystics were all visionaries and if they all produced consistent descriptions of the population of the supernatural world. But visionaries do not agree, and there is no way of even beginning to apply to their reports our ordinary criteria for distinguishing the subjective from the objective; and besides, what a mystic most often comes back with is not a visionary description of a supernatural being that he claims to have observed but rather, highly metaphysical beliefs to the effect that reality is one, that time is unreal and so on.

It seems that mysticism is not at all like using a special sense organ. In 'interior' or 'introvertive' mysticism we abstract away from the senses and discursive thinking and our thought becomes very still, absorbed and undifferentiated. This is not a bit like sense-experience. On the other hand, in the opposite kind of mysticism (variously called 'extravertive', 'panenhenic' or nature-mysticism) we gain a brilliantly-heightened awareness of the external world, not through a special sense but through our ordinary senses. We see the world somewhat as it is seen in the masterpieces of Van Gogh's last eighteeen months.

In both cases a good deal of intellectual interpretation is interwoven with the experience. Thus, an extravertive experience took place on about 1 June 1955 before the great wistaria plant that used to cover a long stretch of buildings in Trinity Great Court, Cambridge. The experience was triggered by the sight in blazing sunshine of a vast wall of teeming azure blossom. The great sweep of blueness suggested eternity, and yet this was the living blue of flowers. So the plant was a symbol of eternal life or of heaven.

The lesson from that example is this: the experience was theory-laden, but we do not first have the experience and then superimpose the interpretation. On the contrary, the interpretation generated the experience. Because the symbolic equation of the blossom with eternal life had already suggested itself unconsciously, the plant appeared charged with supernatural significance – like, perhaps, Van Gogh's irises or sunflowers. But such an experience, intense and moving though it is, cannot be called a direct experience of God through a special sense organ. On the contrary, it was a straightforward perception of a wistaria of outstanding beauty by normal eyesight. In itself the experience, however charged with sacred significance, did not noticeably favour a realist view of God nor provide evidence for the existence of God.

The other main kind of mysticism, the interior or introvertive, is even less like the exercise of a special sense organ and interpretatively even more ambiguous. In the Spring of 1953 a subject experienced several weeks of continuous inner 'warmth'. (It seems to be the case physiologically that in certain religious states body temperature rises.) This unusually sustained period of intense religious happiness was cognitively extraordinarily undifferentiated. Although at the time the subject thought of it as 'the presence of God', and as a continuous umbilical connection with or communion with God, it did not in fact present any given structure.

In general, mystical experience is very common, very diverse, and occurs in every religion and in people of no religion. It is interpretatively highly ambiguous. It certainly does not specially lend itself to a theistic interpretation: on the contrary, so far as there is any consensus or general drift in the testimony it is probably towards monism rather than theism.

There is one kind of religious experience which is firmly theistic in tone, though it is not usually called 'mystical'. I mean the prophetic, numinous experience of God as *other,* as a holy and sovereign will that calls, commands, and puts words in our mouths. To many this is the noblest and most exalted of all forms of religious experience. But it seems to be no longer an authentic religious possibility (see p. 85 below).

The epistemological and the moral arguments for God can be expressed in many different forms, and have not yet attracted so much attention from philosophers as the others that we have already discussed. Sometimes the emphasis in such arguments is more on foundations, and at other times on ideals. Foundation-type arguments see God as the condition of the possibility of knowledge or morality (the world is intelligible because human reason participates in cosmic reason; the world is a fit theatre for the moral life, God's will defines the principles of morality, etc.). In arguments of this kind God is seen as underwriting knowledge or ethics, by setting up the world in such a way as to make them possible and by providing guidelines. There are affinities here with the design argument, as well as with the traditional belief that a human activity is only fully sane and well-ordered when it is conformed to some heavenly archetype.

Now we certainly cannot yet claim to be in possession of a fully satisfactory and generally-agreed autonomous secular theory and justification of either knowledge or morality. To that extent arguments that seek to give some kind of cosmic backing to human knowledge or morality remain theoretically possible. However, they are trying to swim very much against the stream and even if a valid one were to be produced it would not necessarily be theistic in its implications. It might just as well be taken to support, for example, the Stoic or the Taoist views of nature.

The 'ideal' type of argument sees God as providing the final and perfect standard of complete knowledge or moral perfection. We have to suppose, it is claimed, that there is a final truth and an absolute good which is the standard by which all partial truths and lesser goods are ultimately judged. To which the obvious retort is that it is certainly a good thing to hold up before our eyes ideals of complete knowledge and of moral perfection, but we are not obliged to suppose that these ideals are embodied in any actual being. Furthermore, since God's knowledge (being timeless and non-discursive) is usually postulated as being quite different in kind from anything that I can attain to, and God's moral perfection is similarly remote from anything that I can imitate, how do I *benefit* from the supposition that the ideals of knowledge and morality are actualized in God? On the realist view, I cannot attain them in the way that God has attained them, so it does not profit me anything to imagine them actual in God. Surely they would be more effective as purely *human* ideals?

The 'ideal' type of argument from knowledge and morality is therefore again unhelpful to theological realism.

Conclusion From this brief discussion of the traditional arguments for the existence of God I intend to draw only very modest conclusions. It is certainly wrong to say categorically that the arguments are all invalid and the existence of God cannot be proved. You could only say such a thing if the arguments could be stated in definitive forms, and in those forms be conclusively shown to be valid or invalid. Philosophers like to pretend they can achieve this quasi-mathematical precision, but history suggests the opposite. Anselm's ontological argument would seem to be about as short and sharp as one could well expect a substantial philosophical proof to be, and it has often been pronounced stone dead. Yet new formulations of it are still being produced and able people still defend it. Philosophy is done on the basis of a noble lie, a necessary fiction, namely the belief that a thesis can be expressed unambiguously and evaluated conclusively. All the evidence is against it, but one must believe it.

So the history of the debate does not entitle us to conclude with certainty that God's existence is either provable or unprovable. But I suggest that it does indicate some decline of confidence in the proofs and some movement away from theological realism.

A   Anselm's ontological argument is realistic in its implications when and only when it is set against a platonic background. When a modern like Norman Malcolm, who is a follower of Wittgenstein, takes it up it turns out in his hands to have a different and non-realistic meaning.[7]

B   Aquinas' cosmological arguments were also realistic in their original setting, but as time has passed and they have been revised, the emphasis has shifted from God as cause of the world to God as explanation of the world. But given that in this instance we are trying to explain the well-known by the unknown, and given that the facts of evil preclude any hope of showing in detail just how the world is the expression of a loving, all-powerful and all-wise purpose, the sense in which God still does any real explaining (and excludes rival hypotheses) is now minimal. It seems that the argument nowadays expresses an aspiration rather than actually delivers a realistically-conceived God who explains why things are just as they are.

C   The argument from design certainly seems to imply a strongly realistic view of God, but just because it does so it is very vulnerable to criticism. It starts by looking like an empirical hypothesis that proposes God to explain certain facts about the world, but then upon examination it fails to behave like a scientific hypothesis. As the debate proceeds we come to a point where we are very strongly tempted to shift our view, abandon theological realism, and conclude that this kind of belief in God is merely emotive. It expresses awe and gratitude in the face of the wonder of nature, but it has no factual content or explanatory power.

D   Finally, the arguments that begin from premises about religious experience, knowledge and morality do not seem to be particularly friendly to objective or realistic theism. They could just as well be framed so as to lead to monistic or stoic or other conclusions.

David Hume made a similar point about the design argument, in spite of the fact that of all the 'proofs' it seems at first sight to be the one that points most clearly to naive theological realism. On the contrary, said Hume, the premises – for what they are worth – are compatible with a whole variety of fanciful metaphysical hypotheses.[8]

For a very long time philosophical talk about God has been strongly influenced by the traditional theistic arguments. More recently people have said that even if the proofs fail, at least the study of them remains an education in what it means to speak of God. Maybe: but I suggest that it is a more ambiguous education than is usually thought.

3

THE CHARGE OF REDUCTIONISM

It is still not easy to chip away at theological realism without incurring a great deal of hostility and risking charges of reductionism and subjectivism.

Historically, this is rather odd. An excessively intellectualist view of religious beliefs, which sees them simply as making metaphysical assertions, is an aberration typical of the seventeenth and eighteenth centuries. Before that time the old tradition of the negative way and the emphasis on the practical character of religious knowledge helped to check crude realism; and since that time idealism, existentialism and other movements have constantly protested against an over-objectified idea of God.

It has all been of little avail, for a kind of mental inertia brings people swinging back towards realism. In the British debate in this century religious beliefs have repeatedly been seen as metaphysical and have accordingly been criticized by the standard anti-metaphysical arguments of positivism. By the end of the 1950s a few bold spirits began to complain about this systematic misunderstanding of religion. They included T. R. Miles (*Religion and the Scientific Outlook*, 1959), Ninian Smart (*Reasons and Faiths*, 1959) and, a little later, D. Z. Phillips (*The Concept of Prayer*, 1963). Yet in spite of the protests of these and other writers, realism remains strong. It shows itself in the criticism regularly made of modern theologians, that they are betraying the cause they should be defending.

The assumption behind the attack is that a religion is first and foremost a system of beliefs, and that a religious belief-system consists of a set of remarkable claims about what is the case, claims which remain unchanged throughout the history of that religion.

These claims are clear in meaning and if true are of the very greatest importance to us all. Various facts and arguments can count either for or against them, so that the truth of Christianity is a matter on the table for public debate. Everyone knows that the Christian claims do present certain difficulties, for there are many considerations which seem to tell against them. Nevertheless there are at least some counter-arguments, and it is the theologian's job to make as good a case for the defence as he can. What he must not do is to tamper with the claims themselves, for they are constitutive of Christianity. Give them up, and one is no longer talking of the same religion.

Unfortunately — so the critics continue — modern theologians have progressively surrendered the claims. The rot set in with F. D. E. Schleiermacher (1768–1834), the founder of modern theology. Faced with the task of restoring the credibility of Christianity after the devastating criticisms levied against it during the Enlightenment, he began a trend to subjectivism, basing his theology on man, on human feeling and on religious experience, and playing down the old supernaturalism and the great dogmatic affirmations. Since his time liberal theology has constantly tended to reduce Christianity to a set of values and attitudes with hardly any doctrinal underpinning at all. In reaction against it there have been many neo-conservative movements which have tried to reassert the old orthodoxy, but they have not fared noticeably better. The world outside remains incorrigibly secular or naturalistic in outlook and the language of orthodoxy fails to get any grip upon it. Alasdair MacIntyre sums up the situation:

> We can see the harsh dilemma of a would-be contemporary theology. The theologians begin from orthodoxy, but the orthodoxy which has learnt from Kierkegaard and Barth becomes too easily a closed circle, in which believer speaks only to believer. . . . Turning aside from this arid in-group theology, the more perceptive theologians wish to translate what they have to say to an atheistic world. But they are doomed to one of two failures. Either they succeed in their translation: in which case what they find themselves saying has been transformed into the atheism of their hearers. Or they fail in their translation: in which case no one hears what they have to say but themselves.[1]

That quotation is taken from an article in which MacIntyre said that Dr John Robinson, the author of *Honest to God*, was an atheist. According to MacIntyre, you do not believe in God unless you hold that there does really exist a distinct, cosmos-transcending and almighty individual being. So when he translated statements about God into statements about the depths of life, about what is supremely important to us and so on, Robinson was covertly moving over to the atheist position. Robinson kept the word 'God', but he was using it merely as a unifying symbol gathering together those aspects of human experience which are felt to be of the deepest significance to us. Robinson's God is no longer a real individual but just a metaphor for the way certain precious moral intuitions present themselves.

Robinson however refused to admit the charge of atheism. He replied that God is inevitably thought of in different ways in different cultural settings. In primitive prephilosophical thinking God is represented as being 'up there', a superhuman King of Kings enthroned above the highest heaven, and no doubt many people still think of God in that way. Then in metaphysical thinking God was commonly represented as a supernatural being 'out there'. The cosmos was seen as a hierarchy of degrees of reality and power and God was the 'self-existent being,' the most-real being from whom all the grades of finite being are derived and who empowers all subordinate agencies. You could argue back up the chain of being and so prove the existence of the 'necessary', supremely real and powerful being upon whom the whole chain depended.

Such ways of representing the reality of God were, says Robinson, appropriate in earlier periods, and many people are still satisfied with them even today. But to those who have grasped how profoundly secular our own period is the older ways of representing the reality of God have become 'intellectually superfluous, emotionally dispensable and morally intolerable'.[2] The believer must seek a way of projecting or representing the reality of God in a culture for which there is only one world, the world is continuous natural process, and the world exists in human knowledge and experience. In our age, says Robinson, 'We most naturally locate reality, not in another realm, but as the profoundest truth of this one.'[3] And Robinson claims that his reinterpretation of talk about God makes it possible for a fully modern person to reappropriate the riches of the biblical and Christian tradition. On these terms Christianity can continue, whereas if the philosophers are right in insisting on the old supernaturalist interpretation of Christian claims then we shall have to say goodbye to Christianity.

Ironically, many of the strongest advocates of theological realism are philosophers who wish to show that Christianity is not true.

They talk as if the meanings of religious concepts were immutable, like Platonic ideas. They refuse to permit any theological *aggiornamento*. This brings them into a temporary and unholy alliance with conservative believers for whom theological meanings are unchangeable revealed truths. Later on, the philosophers intend to disappoint their allies by saying regretfully that Christianity so understood, though undeniably very impressive, is unfortunately not true. But the conservative believers will then say to themselves, 'Well, the poor philosophers have not the gift of faith, but at least their hearts are in the right place' – and so the alliance is dissolved amicably with each party feeling that it has been profitable, for each of them had his own urgent reasons for wishing to bring about the demolition of liberal theology. It threatened the unbelief of the one and the belief of the other.

Dr Robinson is a churchman and a preacher, and he knows that meanings have changed. To reach a secular audience he is willing to bend meanings further, in order to state Christianity in a form which his hearers may be able to appropriate. If *Honest to God* were really atheistic, it is a little surprising that it should have converted so many people to Christianity.

Besides, even if Robinson's theism is very different from the theism of earlier times, it may still be better to have some religion on Robinson's terms than to have no religion at all. One philosophical critic of modern theology, R. W. Hepburn, himself allows that a religious attitude to life embodies many extremely precious values and experiences which ought not to pass away altogether.[4] If Robinson's type of theology offers a way of salvaging them from the wreckage of the old supranaturalist orthodoxy, then surely we ought to welcome it eagerly?

In any case it is not clear that Robinson's break with tradition is quite so great after all. In philosophy there is a well-known line of argument which says that all our knowledge of the external world is mediated to us by sense-experience. We cannot speak about things as they are absolutely and apart from experience but only of them as they are for us, in experience. So statements about physical objects have to be construed as statements about what can figure in actual or possible human experiences. It is no use complaining that this is 'reductionism', for there is no escape from the argument. Pure empiricism must lead to subjectivism. But a pure empiricist is not trying to alter the human situation, deny the existence of the everyday world, or refuse us the right to talk about physical objects. He is merely pointing out that if experience is to be the criterion – as surely it must be – then it needs to be recognized that our talk about the world of physical objects is talk about them as they are in and for our experience, and we cannot pretend to be able to talk about physical objects as they are absolutely and quite apart from our experience.

Traditional theism said something very similar about God. It always insisted that we have no knowledge of God as he is in himself, for we know God only as he enters into our experience. Talk about God is talk about human experiences, understood as dealings with God or as being effects of God. It is true that Thomas Aquinas, for example, was much more willing than Robinson to try to project the metaphysical existence of God as a distinct world-transcending being, but he was well aware of the difficulty of doing so, and on one vital point he surely agreed with Robinson against the modern philosophers. He did not subordinate religion to theology and he did not take a crudely propositional and intellectualist view of faith. Aquinas' predecessors had been even less inclined than he to make that mistake.

For Robinson religion comes first, and he would I think say that it is an obvious historical fact that the way a religion comes to articulate expression in the language of theology has been highly variable. Indeed, philosophically-articulated accounts of God have been much more diverse than the religious reality of God as attested in devotional writings. Religion is the test of theology and not *vice versa*, to such an extent that one may sometimes find a religious requirement laid upon one flatly to deny a traditional theological claim or assertion.

For example, in a recent book the philosopher Roger Trigg[5] criticizes the late I. T. Ramsey for being perhaps willing to give up the physical resurrection of Christ. All agree that, whatever it means, the resurrection is and has always been regarded as very important in Christianity. Trigg clearly holds that faith in the resurrection of Jesus commits one to holding certain factual beliefs, and he is highly suspicious of Ramsey for saying that someone might believe in the resurrection while denying that the tomb was empty.

Now consider a parallel case: according to the Old Testament God revealed to Moses on Mount Sinai the details of the sacrificial system through which Israel's dealings with God were henceforth to be conducted. So it would seem that an Israelite's communion with God depended – perhaps still depends to this day – upon the truth of certain historical and related claims. The sacrificial system was instituted at a certain date in the past when Israel was gathered at Sinai and Moses climbed the mountain. Those claims give faith its objective anchorage in datable supernaturally-caused events in the past.

Yet strangely enough there were even in Israel some 'subjectivist' or 'liberal' theologians who said that man's inner disposition and commitment to God were of infinitely greater religious importance than the public performance of sacrificial rituals and the belief in their supernatural historical institution. The prophets attacked the cult, internalized and moralized the concept of sacrifice, and rejected the divine institution of the sacrificial system. Jeremiah (7.21ff.) and Amos (5.21–25) actually denied that God had revealed the sacrificial system in the wilderness period. For them, religious inwardness demanded radical theological revision.

Yet at the time a philosopher could surely have complained to Jeremiah, Amos and the rest of them that to reinterpret the concept of sacrifice in terms of human attitudes and dispositions was to use the word in a new subjectivist way quite different from the sense it had always borne in the past, and that to deny the divine institution of the sacrificial system as revealed to Moses was to rob faith of its traditional objectivity.

Nevertheless, and whether philosophers like it or not, religious thought is what it is and not something else, and the kind of move that the prophets made has always been a constitutive part of religious thought. In the Bible it often happens that some people say that a certain institution (the monarchy, the temple, circumcision and so on) was ordained at a specific moment in the past by divine act and promised authority and perpetuity, and then others come along and on *religious* grounds repudiate or qualify those claims. The common pattern is that the old objective institution is superseded and will be replaced by an 'inward' or 'spiritual' equivalent. There will be a new and more inward covenant, a law written on the heart, a circumcision of the heart, a spiritual theocracy (the kingdom of God) to replace the present monarchy, and so on.

Thus the notion that the internalizing of a religious institution or doctrinal theme is a departure from tradition and a betrayal is absurd. On the contrary, the process by which a religious teacher demythologizes and internalizes a traditional belief is familiar within the biblical tradition, and the modern liberal theologian is more 'biblical' (for what that is worth) than his conservative opponent. Thus Yahweh was originally thought of as literally fighting on Israel's side and giving victory in battle, but in the New Testament we find the old theme internalized and so passing into the Christian tradition as the 'spiritual combat', the 'holy war' and the like. In St John's Gospel we find a considerable measure of demythologizing of the traditional eschatological beliefs in the second coming, the last judgment, everlasting life and so on. There is at least a strong tendency to reinterpret all these doctrinal themes in terms of the believer's present religious experience and status before God. In the nineteenth century the theologian F. D. Maurice attempted a similar transformation of the popular eschatology. He was careful to justify the theological moves he was making by appealing extensively to St John, and he also made it clear that he had a specifically religious objection to the standard beliefs in the last judgment and hell, for those beliefs when taken literally have a deleterious effect upon present religious life. Yet careful though Maurice was to establish the biblical basis and the religious motives for his argument, he still attracted just the same sort of literalist criticism as more recent theologians have suffered.

Maurice also applied the same method to the question of the resurrection, though unfortunately (and perhaps partly for reasons of discretion) he wrapped up his argument in such a high-flown rhetorical style that few of his readers can have understood what he was saying.[6] It is clear that he quotes St Paul: 'Flesh and blood cannot inherit the kingdom of God', (I Cor. 15.20) and that he strongly objects to the plain man's carnal and physicalist understanding of the resurrection, but beyond that he is not easy to summarize. Let us put his point more baldly than he does, like this: the religious concern is not for verbal formulae but for a mode of being. The resurrection is a state of the self and a way of living for and from God by the power of God. St Paul, for example, shows no interest either in the mechanics of Jesus' rising or in the empty tomb, which he never even mentions. His thought about the resurrection is intensely communal, participatory and existential. From the religious point of view nothing matters except that believers already participate in Jesus' risen life and must live it out. Preoccupation with Jesus' resurrection as a historical problem (whose evidences are in fact pathetically weak) is ludicrously disproportionate to the world-filling present reality of the resurrection as a power of demand and grace that presently transforms my life. I do know enough of Jesus to connect the resurrection life with him – but not through those evidences. Thus a person who is religiously seized by the risen life might well attack the popular view of Jesus' physical resurrection as a frivolous distraction and as an attempt to evade the present reality and demand of the resurrection.

According to the popular view Christianity has always claimed that the corpse of Jesus was miraculously revived, and in some obscure sense transformed, by a special act of God. Jesus then emerged from the tomb and subsequently showed himself indubitably and physically alive to his followers. But, it is thought, theologians find this account hard to defend in an age of science and historical criticism and so they retreat to a 'merely subjective' view of the resurrection. The theologian is seen as yielding ground and making concessions, conducting a defensive operation.

This popular view entirely misses the religious point, namely that from the religious standpoint truth is subjectivity. Even if the popular view of the resurrection of Jesus were true, how could it ever acquire the power and authority to change my whole life now? A dubiously-evidenced freak event (or even a strongly-evidenced freak event) two thousand years ago is in itself of no religious interest whatsoever.

In the course of the discussion the theologian can make a number of points *ad hominem*. He may point to the true New Testament teaching about the resurrection and he can show the weakness of the traditional historical 'evidences'. More substantially, he may show that the popular view of the resurrection of Jesus is radically incoherent and therefore cannot be true. For it is said of that which the apostles saw both that it was identical with the mortal body of the Jesus who had died and that it was immortal, having conquered death; both that it was a physical object and that it could appear and disappear, pass through locked doors and so on; both that it could eat food and that it was a divinized and heavenly thing: all of which simply does not hang together. If it is replied that admittedly the precise nature of the resurrection is mysterious then one must answer, How can we insist both upon the merits of straightforward realism and upon the mysteriousness of the matter of which we are being exhorted to take a realist view? What is the use of a *mysterious* realism that gives with one hand and takes away with the other?

Yet to make such points – even if only *ad hominem* – may worsen the confusion if it has the effect of locking people into a sterile and quite irreligious debate which never touches the real issue, namely the present religious reality of the resurrection.

These considerations suggest the answer to a question raised by R. W. Hepburn, who criticized the theologian Rudolf Bultmann in an article entitled 'Demythologizing and the problem of Validity'. Hepburn complained that Bultmann repeatedly argues along the following lines:

(a) A fact or argument appears, which *prima facie* is hostile to the validity of the Christian position;

(b) Bultmann turns aside from its negative evidential implication; and

(c) transforms the hostile fact in such a way as to make it yield positive support for a modified and freshly secured theological view.[7]

That complaint by Hepburn suggests that he is dominated by the usual layman's picture of the theologian as a reductionist conducting a sophistical rearguard action bound to end in failure. Later, Hepburn offers a slightly more positive account of what he thinks Bultmann is up to: 'At many crucial points he casts about in his mind for an interpretation of an event which he thinks adequate to the existential seriousness of Christianity, and proceeds to *read back* his interpretation into the original documents.'[8] At least that statement gives Bultmann the credit for having a serious religious concern rather than being a slippery-tongued hack trying to make the best of a bad job; but how does Hepburn know that the greatest of biblical critics is misinterpreting the texts? Hepburn says, 'Bultmann would feel an *embarrassment* at the very possibility that certain events might after all have taken place just as the documents narrate them',[9] for Bultmann is so convinced that the world is a continuous natural process without any divine interventions that nothing can persuade him that one has occurred, or even that the writers of the New Testament really meant to say that one has occurred. But, Hepburn thinks, the New Testament writers did mean to assert that certain events which really had occurred were miraculous events brought about by the direct invention of God. By editing out such ideas in his programme of 'demythologizing', Bultmann arrives at a version of Christianity which has given up all those awkward traditional claims – but in so doing has become unfalsifiable and therefore contentless. Bultmann refuses to make plain 'what states of affairs would be incompatible with Christian belief, or just how different the world would have to be before belief would have to be declared senseless.[10]

This last challenge can be answered straight away. What would falsify Christianity would be a state of affairs in which Christianity had perished *as a religion*. If a time were to come when people no longer found salvation in Christianity, no longer heard a divine call in Jesus' words, no longer experienced conversion through union with Jesus in his death and no longer received the divine spirit, then in that time Christianity would indeed have died. Christianity claims to be saving truth, and if Christianity were to lose the power of salvation it would not be true any more. What else can true religion be but religion through which salvation can be had? Religion is not metaphysics but salvation, and salvation is a state of the self. It has to be appropriated subjectively or existentially. There is no such thing as objective religious truth and there cannot be. The view that religious truth consists in ideological correctness or in the objective correspondence of doctrinal statement with historical and metaphysical fact is a modern aberration, and a product of the decline of religious seriousness.[11] Religious truth is not speculative or descriptive, but practical.

What of the claim that Bultmann reads back his theology into the New Testament? This too is a misunderstanding. Bultmann is careful to distinguish between exegesis, the historical exposition of what the biblical writers meant in their day, and hermeneutics, the way to the religious appropriation of the text by the modern believer. As exegete, Bultmann the historian acknowledges and insists that the world of the New Testament is a supranaturalist world with heavenly beings above and the underworld below, a world of angels, demons, miracles and so on. It was a prescientific and even largely prephilosophical world, and there were people in Greece and Rome then to whom it was almost as queer and remote as it is for us now. A purely historical exegesis of the New Testament would be of no religious value to us today whatever, because the barriers to its appropriation by us are too great. That is why fundamentalist and ultra-conservative styles of religion are now so completely bankrupt. They require so much self-deception as to corrupt the soul.

Hermeneutics, then, will be a theory to justify and a method for carrying out the authentic appropriation by the modern believer of the religious realities to which the New Testament bears witness.

At this point I have to diverge from Bultmann because I think he and Robinson and many others have somewhat confused the issue. The task is to overthrow a religiously bankrupt, because falsely objectified, dogmatism and to put specifically religious categories at the centre. The task is *not* to move from an objective and god-centred theology to a man-centred theology, as has too often happened. It is not primarily a matter of putting man and human psychology at the centre, but rather of putting the religious and the demand for its subjective appropriation by us at the centre.

To return to the problem of hermeneutics, there are overwhelmingly strong reasons of a scientific kind for supposing that in first-century Palestine the laws of nature were just the same as they are now and the world worked just as it does now. Miracles no more happened then than they do today. Why then did the New Testament writers write as they did? The answer is well known. In that sort of culture belief moulded perception, and the language of religious expression was not clearly distinguished from the language of exact description. In our culture we have learnt that if you are going to use language as an efficient and powerful tool for describing, explaining and predicting it must not at the same time be doing anything else but must be quite neutral so far as questions of morality, religion and culture are concerned. We have become aware that different kinds of language have to be used to do different kinds of job. Prescientific men conflated the different functions of language, for example by projecting their local cultural beliefs into their description of events and their account of the nature of the universe, whereas our natural science is the same in every country whatever the local religion or ideology may be.

Now suppose we ask, did St Paul think the resurrection of Jesus was a fact? The answer can only be, No, because St Paul did not have our concept of a fact. Influenced by modern scientific and critical ways of thinking, we use the word 'fact' of descriptive propositions whose truth is testable in ways quite independent of local cultural beliefs, human wishes and so on. Our concept of a fact is the concept of a truth which is religiously and morally neutral. Not only did St Paul not have that concept, but even if he had had it, it would have been quite inappropriate to the resurrection, for he certainly did not think of the resurrection as a religiously-neutral occurrence which could be discussed quite apart from whether anyone believed it and quite apart from its religious claim upon one who heard of it.

Once we grasp this point we need not be distracted by all the debates about demythologization, existentialist interpretation, subjectivism and so on. The crucial point is to grasp the differences between the use of language in a prescientific – and even largely prephilosophical – cultural setting, and the uses of language in the modern West.

The conclusion is clear. As a matter of historically-correct exegesis we have to recognize that for the early Christians and for many subsequent centuries the resurrection was a reality expressible in a kind of language that blended quasi-factual assertion and religious participation, a kind of language which we do not have any more because we now express facts in the worlds of nature and history in a special kind of descriptive language purged of local religious and cultural associations.

In ancient Palestine there was no scientific, objectified history or factuality. There was only history as mythological reality, history as a community's sense of itself. We now live in an age which sharply separates factual description from religious expression, so we no longer have the old kind of mixed or confused style of speaking available to us. How are we to speak of the resurrection? Not factually or objectively; for if like some eighteenth-century apologists we try to establish the resurrection as an objective historical fact we shall – even if we succeed – end with something religiously worthless that can never acquire the power to change my whole life.

The crucial objection to religious realism is that insofar as it succeeds in being realistic it necessarily ceases to be religious. The modern notions of fact, truth and so on are religiously neutral, so that insofar as an apologist manages to establish a realist interpretation of some major doctrine he necessarily destroys it as religion.

Today, the factual is non-religious. What are the implications of the converse, that religion is non-factual? The New Testament is a religious book, and hermeneutics is an attempt to appropriate its religious meaning. So the resurrection is a religious reality – that is, a state of the self and a form of salvation – which according to the New Testament was introduced by Jesus or which arrived with him. It means the state of salvation towards which the Jewish religion is oriented, now attained by Jesus and available (by anticipation, as it were) to his followers. It consists in the maximal degree of liberation from the power of evil and of spiritual individuation, creativity and responsiveness. The enjoyment of this through Jesus is, by definition, faith in his resurrection. Compared with this tremendous religious reality, 'historical' claims about walking corpses and empty tombs are foolish and irrelevant.

4

CREATION AND THEOLOGICAL REALISM

I have been combatting the view – typical of the eighteenth-century debate about miracles, but still very common – that someone who professes Christian faith is committed to claiming that certain extraordinary, supernaturally-caused events happened in the past. His present faith is thought to be justified insofar as good arguments can be mustered to show that those remarkable events really did happen.

The most often-quoted case is that of the resurrection, which everyone agrees to be a central and constitutive theme in Christianity. I have objected to the false intellectualism of the popular view, saying that the resurrection is a presently-available religious reality, namely the risen life lived by those who are risen with Jesus; that is, who have followed a certain pattern of religious action. Through baptism and conversion they have been reborn to a new life which is lived 'from God'. This new life is historically traceable to the impact of Jesus' life and death, but it is absurd to claim that it depends upon the truth of any assertions about the mechanics of Jesus' resurrection. If his words and witness teach me an effective pattern of religious action, or holy Way, and if by religiously appropriating to myself what he shows I am God's in union with Jesus, then I am entitled to say that he is God's; but there is no need at all to say any more than that. To see the resurrection as primarily a past historical event is superstitious and irreligious, for it deflects attention away from the immediate religious demand that I must appropriate and live the resurrection myself today. The mysteries of faith must not be intellectualized, objectified, and debated as if they were abnormal occurrences of

the sort which fascinate occultists. The resurrection is not a supernatural occurrence but something I must do and share.

You may be willing to concede this point, but I can imagine that
you still suspect me of 'subjectivism' and wish to point out that I
cannot by manoeuvres of this kind evade the necessity to make and
to justify metaphysical claims about God.

The *prima facie* case runs like this: the way someone who believes in God talks about God shows that he thinks God really
exists independently of faith. The believer shows by the way he
talks of God that, for him, he himself and all other things depend
for their very being upon God's creative will. What is more, a god
is always a Lord, one with authority and power over events. The
believer who insists that there is only one God must attribute to
that God sole and complete control over all that happens. A God
that is not sovereign is no God. So religious faith in God is indissolubly bound up with a set of assertions about God's existence
and activity in creation and providence.

Yet, surprisingly, this straightforward view of the matter will
not stand up to close examination. We can move in upon it and
break it up from several different starting-points, and in so doing
we will begin, just begin, to see the shape of something quite
different and much more interesting.

The first line of argument starts from the recognition that there
are two fundamentally different accounts of creation, which have
rarely been properly distinguished from each other and so do not
have generally-agreed names. I shall call them the *mythological*
and the *monotheistic* accounts.

The mythological account of creation is offered as an explanation of the origin and maintenance of the cosmic order. It seems
that so far back as we can make out people in traditional societies
always believed in a graded hierarchy of supernatural beings influ-
encing events at different levels in the cosmos. The highest beings
with the greatest power and authority were naturally linked with
the heavens, which show the greatest degree of regularity, im-
mensity and perfection. By contrast, the lower levels of the cosmos,
the ungovernable sea and the depths of the earth, are relatively
unformed and chaotic. They were the province of low-ranking and
capricious or even malignant spirits.

A great many peoples still either believe or formerly believed in
a supreme God or high God, an ethical Sky-Father who is the
highest power in the cosmos and the ultimate source of the moral
order. But across the world there has been a very widespread

tendency for the Sky-Father in particular, and the oldest generation of gods in general, to retire into obscurity and be forgotten. Just because he is so universal, wise and passively unchangeable the Sky-Father tends to be kicked upstairs and made ineffectual by the rise of a younger generation of more vigorous deities.[1] They make him redundant.

In monotheism, of course, this is prevented from happening by the drastic demotion of all heavenly beings other than the one God. The first serious attempt to depose God was also the last – that made by Lucifer, or Satan. It could not possibly succeed and was dramatically punished.

When the Israelites developed their early myths and theology of creation, and in particular the two celebrated myths in Genesis which have so deeply influenced all subsequent thought, they certainly considerably revised the more archaic ways of thinking that they received. Nevertheless, a number of features of the traditional mythological world-view were preserved and transmitted to future generations.

First, creation was pictured as an event, which took place 'in the beginning'.

Secondly, the created world was seen as a divinely constituted and therefore unchangeable order. As in all traditional societies that do not recognize the possibility of fundamental historical change, it was supposed that the basic moral relations between man and woman, parents and children, men and animals, and so forth were fixed by God in the beginning and remain thereafter forever unalterable.

So thirdly, there remained a strong tendency to sacralize the cosmos. Though it has been much cut down in elaboration, the principle still holds that higher-ranking things in the universe energize or activate lower-ranking things. The universe is a plenum, a complete and immutable chain of beings ranging from the lowest to the highest degree of reality and perfection. The heavens are more perfect than the earth and all form, power and order are thought of as coming down from the heavens, from God through various intermediary messengers and ministers of his court.

Fourthly, this way of thinking gives a way of conceiving the greatness and the reality of God, and the mode of God's existence. Creation is a system of arrows pointing to God. The graded series of degrees of power in the cosmos points up to the supreme power of God. The hierarchy of degrees of reality in the cosmos points to the supreme reality of God. The hierarchy of degrees of permanence and stability in the cosmos points up to the unchangeableness of God – and so on. All the spokes point towards the hub.

Fifthly, animistic explanation is retained and is still felt to be useful and informative. Why is something so? – because God so willed it. Why is such and such happening? – a good or an evil spirit, as the case may be, is responsible.

When creation is thought of in this way it is seen as a refracted image of God, or as a many-coloured display of God. God is integral to the way the cosmos is seen, for he is its coping-stone. To change the metaphor, the throne of God is the hook from which the entire chain of being hangs. It is possible to 'prove' the existence of God by arguing up the degrees of being towards the supreme, independent and self-existent being from which all things depend. Since causality is seen as the communication of being from the greater to the lesser, there can be causal arguments back and up to the first cause of all things.

This way of thinking, prolonged in neoplatonic and Christian Aristotelian philosophy, survived until quite recently. Yet alongside it can also be found developing another and much more uncompromisingly monotheistic account. Rudolf Bultmann contrasts the two ways of thinking about creation in the following passage, where he claims that St Paul (I Cor. 8.6) does *not* have in mind

> . . . a theoretical world-view that holds that human existence is to be referred back to the existence of God as its cause or substance and that because our existence stems from his it is endowed with his nature, so that we now bear divine being within us. Rather it means, first of all, that we are creatures, that we are dust and ashes, that in ourselves we are nothing. It means that in ourselves we have no permanence and nothing whereupon we could base our own right and our own claims, nothing that we ourselves can assert as the meaning and worth of our life. We are encompassed by the same nothingness that encompasses the entire creation; we are suspended in nothing.[2]

Bultmann insists that there is no way from the world to God. For him the meaning of the doctrine of creation *ex nihilo*, out of nothing, is that creatures are in themselves religiously worthless, 'nothing'. The man who believes in God as creator, says Luther, 'must be dead to everything, to good and bad, to death and life, to hell and heaven, and must confess in his own heart that he is able to do nothing by his own power.' Bultmann adds, 'God creates out of nothing, and whoever becomes nothing before him is made

alive',[3] so that the only way to know God as creator is to die with
Christ on the cross and by God be raised from death or nothingness. Bultmann's account implies that when believers say things
like, 'God gives all good things, God is maker of all things, life is
a gift', they are not stating a theory about the world's origin but
using language expressively on the basis of their experience of
resurrection. Talk of creation expresses what it feels like to have
been re-made through faith.

It is evident that Bultmann completely rejects the mythological
account of creation that we described earlier, and it is easy to
assume that he is doing this as part of the usual theologians'
rearguard action. The scientific revolution replaced animistic explanation with new and far more powerful mechanistic styles of
explanation, and the old mythological view of the world as a sacred
cosmos was finally overthrown. Religious, symbolic and ethical
meanings were expelled from nature. So when Bultmann says that
the creature is in itself destitute of religious significance (or
'nothing', in the traditional rhetoric) he is making a virtue out of
necessity. After the scientific revolution faith had to retreat within
the self and become internalized in order to survive at all.

Simply to see the matter in those terms, however, is to ignore
the positive religious motives and deep historical roots of
Bultmann's point of view. To a theist there are obvious religious
objections to the 'mythological' account of creation. Its doctrine
of degrees of being, perfection and activity puts God and creatures
on a common scale and so approximates to the emanationist doctrines against which early Christianity fought.[4] From the outset
Gnosticism was perceived as a deadly enemy, and the mythological
view of creation, with its various hierarchies pointing up to God,
is very close to Gnosticism. If you regard God as the explanation
of the world, suppose there to be causal relations between God
and the world, and regard the perfections of creatures as so many
varying degrees of participation in the divine perfection, you run
very close to viewing God as part of the world, or at least to
viewing God and the world as together components of a great
totality. To avoid these errors and to maintain the divine transcendence it was insisted that all creatures are immediately posited by
God's inscrutable and incomprehensible will. But this shatters all
rationally-apprehensible connections between God and the world
and so makes the mode of God's existence quite inconceivable. As
a Russian Orthodox writer admirably puts it:

All creatures are balanced upon the creative word of God, as if upon a bridge of diamond; above them is the abyss of the divine infinitude, below them that of their own nothingness.[5]

All creatures are alike 'nothing'. This means that there are no ladders from creatures to God. There are no theologically significant differences of perfection among creatures such that they can be arranged in a series ascending to the divine reality. The divine infinitude and creatures are in no way commensurable. There is therefore no analogy of being and no way in which, starting from premises about the world, one could hope to ascend to the knowledge of God or say anything at all about the mode of the divine existence. So Philaret's statement about creation in effect becomes strongly world-denying. What he means is, 'Think only of God, and of your own nothingness before God!' Thus he approaches Bultmann's view. On the mythological account, talk of creation is richly descriptive; but on this other account its function is to express certain spiritual attitudes and aspirations. 'I am created out of nothing' means, and means only, 'God is everything to me, and I am nothing before God.'

Here then are two very different ways of thinking about God and creation which have from the beginning existed side by side in the Christian tradition. I called them mythological and monotheistic, and it is evident by now that they correspond more or less to the affirmative and negative ways in spirituality. The negative way attempts to do justice to God's transcendence but at the price of making God unknowable. Religious language then perforce becomes expressive, not descriptive, and the relation to God has to be enacted in spirituality because it can in no way be articulated in knowledge. A high and orthodox emphasis on the divine transcendence forces me in the end to a non-cognitive or (as people say) 'subjectivist' philosophy of religion. The 'higher' God is the more inward God is, and the less we know of him the more he makes us grow spiritually.

Alternatively, the affirmative way sees the world as full of images of God and hierarchies pointing to God, but insofar as it moves from the world to God by some sort of extrapolation it can only arrive at an idol and not the true God. By loosely combining the two ways – in spite of the fact that they are really incommensurable – Christian theology has at some stages in its history given the impression that it is possible to say what kind of existence or reality it is that God is thought to have. But it is not, for what has happened in modern times is that the development of the scientific world-picture has annihilated the mythological way of seeing the world as creation, exposing its ideas of causality, of degrees of being and so forth as absurd. Now only the negative way is left, but the negative way does not leave one with any means of saying just what kind of being or reality it is that God has. Its language is inevitably expressive and not descriptive.

It is clear that so far as the doctrine of creation is concerned it is not a simple matter of believers making clearcut claims on the one side versus agnostics on the other. On the contrary, believers find themselves constrained by strong pressures towards agnosticim that arise within religious language itself.

The language of prayer and providence provides further examples of these pressures. It is not just that under secular scientific or empiricist criticism believers retreat from descriptive, assertion-making language to attitude-expressing language, true though that may be in its own way; what is more significant is that internal considerations within the proper movement of the religious life compel us to move from assertorial to expressive ways of talking.

In the case of prayer, no doubt we all begin from the idea that prayer is a method of obtaining what we desire by asking God for it in a sufficiently persuasive way. The vocabulary of prayer shows it: offer petitions, intercede, request, beg, beseech, implore, hear and answer, attend, hearken, give heed, and so on. We start from some kind of confidence that prayer 'works' and we do not pray in vain, but we are all familiar with the qualifications and counter-arguments – of a religious kind – which soon have to be reckoned with.

'God is said to be unchangeable, so is it not absurd to imagine that we should attempt to change the will of the maker of the world?' Answer: your prayers and their answers are both of them already foreordained, so that in praying you do not alter the plan, you implement it.[6]

'Surely it is impious to use my relation to God as a means of obtaining various goods for myself; and how can I pray for happiness when Christianity is a gospel of suffering? On the other hand it seems presumptuous to pray expressly for suffering, and perhaps even a little mad. So what can I pray, except that God's will be done?'[7]

'How can I tell God what is best for people? Surely, by definition God knows what is best, knows it before I ask him, and knows

better than I whether and when a particular boon should be given'
(see Matt. 6.8).

By the time we have digested these and other familiar points, we
have ceased to see prayer as causally efficacious. Religious thought
itself forces us towards a purely expressive view of intercession.
The act of praying for someone is not a quasi-technical operation,
but a ritual expression of love and hope and concern. When I pray
for someone I think lovingly of him before God and commend him
to God. It would be impious and foolish to suppose that I had the
power to manipulate God or to coerce God, or that God needs
information, or waits for encouragement from me before he acts.

Islam, as is well known, drastically restricts the place of intercession in religious practice, for the reasons we have sketched.

The case of belief in providence is rather more complicated.
There can be no doubt that the starting point is again a form of
naive realism. One who believes in providence believes that his life
is watched over and guided. He believes that the whole course of
things is supervised and is being directed towards a supremely good
end.

The language used suggests the image of an adult who supervises
young children at play, making sure no one is injured, soothing
hurt feelings, comforting the tearful and so on. However, people
who believe in providence seem to accept that many evil things and
many serious accidents do nevertheless happen, and God does not
intervene to prevent them from occurring. So what do they mean?
Believers reply, 'My faith in providence rests on experiences of
being helped, experiences of things turning out unexpectedly well,
on happy coincidences, and on certain specially revelatory events
such as Jesus' life, death and resurrection.'

These scraps are comparatively small things to set in the balance
against the vast and appalling evils of twentieth-century history,
are they not? Surely we cannot suppose that a factual claim is
being made? One indication that the claim is not factual is that
faith is often most highly commended and is most distinctively
itself precisely when it is most counterfactual, when one doggedly
trusts God in the hardest times. The victory of faith is not its
confirmation by the facts but its triumph over them.

Here are a few examples from the Old Testament. When his
brothers are nervous about Joseph's favour he says to them, 'You
meant evil against me; but God meant it for good, to bring it about
that many people should be kept alive, as they are today'
(Gen. 50.20, RSV). Joseph here could be read as proposing an

hypothesis to account for a fortunate coincidence, and that is no doubt how most people do understand what he says. But suppose we had said to him, 'You are being irrational. It is much more common for people in sore straits not to be unexpectedly helped out. Do a count, and you'll soon realize that statistically the evidence against a good providence is much stronger than the evidence for it.' If we had said this to him, Joseph would surely have replied that he spontaneously desired to thank God on this occasion and had not for a moment thought of totting up the evidence in a scientific way. But that suggests that Joseph was talking expressively rather than descriptively.

Now consider what Shadrach, Mesach and Abednego say to King Nebuchadnezzar when he threatens them with the fiery furnace if they will not worship his golden image: 'Our God whom we serve is able to deliver us from the burning fiery furnace; and he will deliver us out of your hand, O king. But if not, be it known to you, O king, that we will not serve your gods or worship the golden image' (Dan. 3.17f.). Here faith resolves to cling to God regardless of how the facts turn out, in a story clearly intended to be edificatory. At this moment faith is undeniably ceasing to be any kind of empirical generalization from experience and becoming something expressive, a religious attitude to experience maintained uncompromisingly come what may.

It should be clear that by 'expressive' I do not mean 'emotive'. Rather, the point is that to believe in God is simply to declare an intention to be loyal to religious values whatever happens. That faith is not really a generalization from the facts nor a hypothesis to account for the facts, but on the contrary a power of defying and triumphing over adverse fact, is shown in this splendid statement from Habbakuk:

> Though the fig tree do not blossom,
>   nor fruit be on the vines,
> the produce of the olive fail
>   and the fields yield no food,
> the flock be cut off from the fold
>   and there be no herd in the stalls,
> yet I will rejoice in the LORD,
>   I will joy in the God of my salvation.
>   (Hab. 3.17f.)

Faith is most distinctively itself when it gives the individual the courage to be victorious in adversity: 'Who shall separate us from the love of Christ? Shall tribulation, or distress, or persecution, or famine, or nakedness, or peril, or sword?.... No, in all these things we are more than conquerors through him who loved us' (Rom. 8.35, 37).

If faith in divine providence were the empirical belief that at least the great majority of good people have happy endings, and at least the great majority of bad people come to sticky ends, then one can only say that such a belief is too absurd for anyone to hold and too absurd for anyone to think it worth checking by systematic counting. Faith in divine providence is not a factual belief from which we can deduce predictions about the future course of human history. On past form there seems little profit in claiming that God will not permit mass starvation or the use of nuclear weapons, for example. Faith in divine providence does not empower us to say with confidence that certain evils will not be allowed to happen. What faith does entitle us to say is that we will survive, we will come through and evil will not have the final word. Faith in God is itself a way of overcoming evil and not a theory that evil will be overcome quite apart from faith.

In summary, in confessing God as creator I testify to my experience of rebirth and renewal insofar as the religious concern and religious values really have come to take first place in my life. Faith in divine providence expresses my conviction that if I am unflinchingly loyal to this concern and these values they will not fail me.

5

WORSHIP AND THEOLOGICAL REALISM

The main controversy in religious thought today is one about the meaning of religious beliefs, the level at which they are to be understood. Now that we have moved into a largely non-religious era we do not find it easy to understand faith. Is it making factual claims or not? This question divides the realists, who comprise conservative believers and a large number of sceptics, from the expressivists, who are believers seeking an alternative account.[1]

The realists stick to what they say is commonsense and tradition. They say that the existence of God is in the end a factual question. One who believes in God must maintain that there exists a certain distinct and independent individual Spirit, the creator and ruler of all things, unsurpassable in power, wisdom and goodness, who would exist and be exactly the same even if nobody believed in him any longer and even if there were no world at all. On the realist view, believers must make metaphysical claims.

Realism is a doctrine about the *meaning* of talk about God, which is why it is held by sceptics. If you are to count as a believer in God, say the sceptics, then that is what you have to believe. Sceptics are fond of laying down the law in this way.

The other group, the expressivists, hold that the God of realism does not in fact exist but is an illusion created by a misunderstanding of the nature of religious language. They hold that religious language is basically expressive in force, not descriptive. God's reality is not a matter of facts and evidence, but of the unconditional authority of religious categories in a person's life. Religious faith is not a quasi-scientific theory about how the world works and who is running things behind the scenes. For suppose that we were to debate the matter and to conclude that it is after all a plausible theory that there exists a cosmic supermind: how could this hypothesis ever acquire the authority to change my whole life? No, the word 'God' does not refer to an entity that is supposed to exist quite apart from the practice of religion and is invoked to explain why things happen as they do. Rather, the meaning of the word 'God' shows itself in the practice of religion as a way of appraising one's own life and of responding to the fact that the world is what it is.

Realists emphasize the objective existence of God and God's control over the world. Their view of religion is cosmological and they reckon to have the tradition on their side. The expressivists, by contrast, take a highly internalized view of faith. They stand in the long tradition that rejects any alliance of the gospel with Greek philosophy. In particular they stand in the tradition of Lutheranism, pietism, methodism and Christian existentialism. For them Christianity is not a cosmic hypothesis nor a theory about the world but a categorical demand that one should change one's whole life. Interpreting religion in cosmological and objective terms is, they say, at best superstitition and at worst sin, for it deflects attention away from the inner demand which is the essence of religion.

It sounds as if the realists are saying that when we talk of God we speak of an object that really exists or is supposed to exist, whereas the expressivists regard God as a purely ideal or imaginary being. So, it may be thought, the expressivists are people who wish to continue practising religion although they no longer actually believe there is a God.

However, this way of putting it is unfair, and the expressivists deny that they are atheists. They say that the sense in which mathematical objects like numbers 'exist' is given in the way mathematicians talk about numbers, and the sense in which physical objects like chairs exist is given in the way we talk about physical objects. Similarly, the sense in which God is real is given in the language and practice of religion.

Now in pre-critical philosophy it was quaintly supposed that you could arrange these different senses of reality or existence on a continuous scale, with God at the top. But modern philosophy has abandoned that idea and says merely that words like 'reality' or 'existence' are used in different and incommensurable ways in different contexts. There is no point in losing sleep over the reality of numbers. The sense in which numbers are real becomes apparent in the practice of mathematics. As for God, his reality is said to be eternal and unchangeable. This should surely warn us that God is not supposed to exist as things in the world of experience exist. God's reality is unique in kind. What it is is given in, and shows itself in, the practice of religion.

The realists are not at all satisfied with this explanation and indeed the two parties detest each other's views. Are they then quite irreconcilable? There is one possibility of mediation. Since the realists appeal to tradition as supporting their interpretation, and the expressivists for their part appeal to religious practices such as worship, prayer and the spiritual life, we ought surely to be able to resolve or at least to clarify the issue between them by considering the traditional practice of worship. For worship is the formal act of expressing in words and gestures what God is and how we stand before God, and it has the great advantage of being a public activity that follows a prescribed form. It is on record, and available for objective study by the analysis of its speech-acts and the interpretation of its gestures. It ought then to be possible to demonstrate from people's liturgical practice in just what sense God is real to them, and what is shown about God by the way people do business with God in the liturgy.

Unfortunately there is a snag here, for official forms of worship may not always be a reliable guide to current beliefs. In the Book of Common Prayer the Commination Service is still ordered to be read on Ash Wednesday. It contains an impressive series of ritual imprecations, declarations of God's curse upon various rather obscure species of sin; but it would be unwise to assume that your parish priest – or even the Church of England in general – still holds the beliefs about God that are clearly implied in the service. Ritual practices often survive long after the beliefs they imply have been repudiated or forgotten and perhaps overlaid with later allegorical interpretations. Occasionally there is a revolt, with reformers complaining that current ritual practice embodies archaic, ugly and defective ideas about God; but what more often happens is that there is a gradual process of reinterpretation by the internalization and moralization of religious ideas. The most familiar example is the development from human sacrifice to animal sacrifice, to linguistic acts expressing self-surrender to God in faith – 'the calves of our lips' – and finally the complete moralization of sacrifice as it acquires its modern meaning of altruistic conduct.

In this development the ancient language and images are often retained under the later superimposed reinterpretations. For example we still hear the story of Abraham and Isaac read in church.

Sermons are preached on it and Kierkegaard based a book on it.[2] In practice the story is nowadays tacitly assumed to be about faith, and at another level is taken to symbolize the sacrifice of Christ. Believers would certainly reject, if it were put to them, the suggestion that they approve of a plan to sacrifice a child. Nevertheless Christian worship does keep alive the idea of human sacrifice, and someone studying the words used in worship might easily make the mistake of imputing to Christians much cruder beliefs than in fact they hold. We have to be wary of assuming that people's beliefs are as realistic as the language of their worship.

However, it is not just a matter of modern believers having allegorized away archaic and crude ideas. Those old meanings really are still present. For example, the sign of the cross was probably originally an apotropaic gesture warding off evil powers. The modern believer may say that he has no views about evil spirits and makes the sign of the cross simply as a ritual expression of his self-surrender to God after the pattern of the cross of Jesus. But influential modern theories in social and psychological science encourage us to suppose that, whatever people may protest to the contrary, the deep meaning is somehow the *real* meaning. The person who makes the sign of the cross may profess the modern internalized meaning, but a psychologist will retort, 'So you say, but really your gesture shows that deep down you are still afraid of evil spirits. That the sign of the cross is really a magical action intended to ward off evil spirits can be shown historically, and is proved by the fact that in ghost stories and horror films everyone instantly recognizes it as such.'

The problem is that religious practice, being a reflection and a projection of human nature, resembles it in having an id as well as a superego. The id of religion is its archaic, gross, magical, irrational and anthropomorphic meaning, still very evident in its rituals. The superego of religion is the cleaned-up, moralized and reinterpreted meaning that has been superimposed. At different levels in the psyche both survive.

It is striking that in modern times there has been such a strong reaffirmation of the id of religion. Freud himself led the way, for he notoriously thought little of the philosophy of religion and modern liberal theology. His mind was always drawn to the id of religion. He gave in the end a reductive explanation of it but he respected it as something of real power. Freud had no time for the God of the philosophers but in his own way he admired the ferocious, rampaging old patriarch who lurks somewhere at the back

AUGUSTANA UNIVERSITY COLLEGE LIBRARY

of theistic belief.[3] And in recent years at least some religious conservatives have been sophisticated enough to ally themselves with
Freud and reaffirm old 'realistic' and mythological ideas in the
name of objectivity. So they will say that it is more objective to
regard the resurrection as the restoration to life of Jesus' corpse,
more objective to claim that in the eucharist believers really do eat
the body and blood of Christ, and objective to see Jesus' death as
a cosmic sacrifice. Like Freud the religious conservative wishes to
reaffirm the more archaic levels of religious meaning, and since
they are indeed still present in the language and gestures of the
liturgy it is hard to deny him the right to do it.

What are his motives? Historically, it seems that he is replying
ad hominem to all those sceptics who point out parallels between
Christianity and various themes in folklore and primitive religion.
'Yes', he says, 'Christianity is universal and it is incarnational –
which means carnal. It is only to be expected that you should find
in Christian worship everything from cannibalism to pure intellectual mysticism. Everything that is in human nature is represented
in Christian worship.' So he is willing freely to acknowledge the
gross and archaic element in worship – while at the same time
other worshippers may be allegorizing the same ideas and understanding them purely ethically. All of which makes the interpretation of worship a much more uncertain business than at first
appears.

In his book *The Concept of Worship*[4] Ninian Smart offers a
clear analysis of the central ideas involved in worship which strongly suggests a realist interpretation of belief in God. One who
worships bows down. His words and gestures closely resemble
those that might have been used in presenting a petition to a king,
homage to a lord, or a gift to a chief. A modern illustration is the
act of saluting in the Army. The junior salutes first in token of
respect, and the superior returns the salute in an acknowledgment
which carries a faint suggestion of benediction. Both are gratified
because the social order has been confirmed; due respect has been
paid and grace has been bestowed. Had the junior failed to salute
his omission would have been regarded as a potentially threatening
revolt against due order, and the superior would have restored the
status quo and his own wounded honour by rebuking the inferior
with considerable force. In that case the inferior should unflinchingly accept the rebuke because it puts things right.

The dynamics of worship are undoubtedly very similar. God
must be given his due, and in return he bestows forgiveness, grace,

and a blessing at the end of the act of worship. But if God is not given his due he will be obliged to vindicate his name by putting the offenders down forcefully. God seems to stand to the world in general and to believers in particular in much the same relation as that between an old-fashioned absolute monarch and his subjects, for God is King of Kings and Lord of Lords.

Our first impression of the language of worship, then, is that it does embody a very definitely realistic and indeed anthropomorphic view of God. Material drawn from human social relations is adapted and used by the community to relate itself to God. But our previous discussion has warned us that religious symbolism is many-levelled and can be interpreted in many ways. Further analysis of worship confirms its socially-conditioned character and at the same time begins to introduce various qualifications.

First we notice that the deity is not present in just the same way as a king giving audience is present. Human gestures of bowing down and the like have to be oriented in a certain direction, and so various symbol-systems come to be set up which create arrows or perspectives along which worship is directed towards God. There are graded series of holy seasons, places, persons and images which direct worship towards its unseen and transcendent focus. But although the symbolism may give the uninitiated the impression that whatever is being used as a pointer to the divine presence is itself being worshipped as an idol, there are no genuine idolaters. On the contrary, we commonly find that within the religious traditions there are well-remembered warnings against taking the symbolism too 'literally'. As King Solomon says to God when dedicating the Temple, 'Heaven and the highest heaven cannot contain thee; how much less this house which I have built' (I Kings 8.27). The more we explore the extravagant richness of religious symbolism the more we also encounter warnings against being misled by it.

Secondly, a similar point has to be made about the extraordinary variety and complex logic of ritual action. At first glance it seems very dramatic and realistic, but on reflection we are obliged to reverse our verdict.

There is no doubt about the verbal ornateness and elaboration of worship. Although they have never been fully analysed, there are probably hundreds of distinct linguistic ritual acts and their ordering in sequence gives to worship a strongly dramatic character.

Thus in *opening* an act of worship the priest may call upon the worshippers (invitation, salutation, exhortation), and the worshippers may call the deity (invocation, adjuration, conjuration). There may be direct, abrupt address to the deity (exclamation, ejaculations, alerting and 'arrow' prayers and gestures) or more formal gestures such as lustrations and other purificatory rites and prayers, and acts of homage, bowing down, or prostration.

Forms of *praise* include benediction of God, commemoration, recitation, creed and profession, thanksgiving, acclamation, adoration and ascription.

God may be called upon for *forgiveness and help* in ways that include confession and plea, acts of contrition, penance and expiation, and promises to abjure and renounce. More forcefully, there may be lamentation, apologia, wrestling and attempts at persuasion by flattery, reproach, cajoling and even threat. Supplication, petition and intercession may take many forms: the English Litany, for example, includes long series of invocations, deprecations, obsecrations, suffrages and collects.

The greatest variety of all is in the area of *promise and change of status*, and one can only list a few forms: vow, covenant, pledge, devotion, charge, threat, imprecation, pronouncement, declaration, consecration, dedication, sanctification, affirmation, spell, and the whole range of sacramental and related actions such as baptizing, ordaining, insufflation, unction, marrying, exorcism, habiting and so on.

Finally, in *closing* an act of worship we may find such forms as commendation, benediction, doxology, the Amen, valediction and simple dismissal.

These various linguistic acts and gestures are not all addressed to God. God answers back, speaking words of absolution or blessing through the mouth of the priest or revealing himself in warning, command and promise in the reading of the scriptures and the sermon. There may also be some dialogue of various sorts between different members of the human congregation, as in antiphonal recitation, or in salutation and response.

It seems then that liturgical action is a drama. It is not merely enacted before God, as if God were an invisible spectator whom the players hope to please by their performance. On the contrary, God takes an active part. God is incorporated into a complex human social interchange. Does not this again suggest that the practice of worship implies a vividly realistic and anthromorphic view of God?

No, it does not; for what is really significant about worship is how very formal it is. An English idiom reminds us that one worships 'from afar'. The extreme dramatic ornateness and formality of worship carries a message about the distance and the inscrutability of the gods, and if we can decode the message we may glimpse behind it a clue to the nature of the gods which will take us a long way from naive realism.

Many ancient mythologies suggest that in the beginning gods and men, immortals and mortals, mingled in easy fellowship. Formal worship was not necessary because heaven and earth were not sharply distinct realms. However, the gods always had greater wisdom and power and were free to withdraw when they wished, and a time came when, for whatever reason, heaven and earth drew apart and the old intimacy was lost. They were now more enigmatic and their favour was harder to win. Worship perforce became more ceremonious and tinged with a certain anxiety. Things were not as easy as they had formerly been for the gods were further off, whether because man had fallen or the gods had risen.

The fascination of Homer for later readers lies in the fact that he pitches his narrative in the time of transition between these two states of religion. The gods still appear in human form and there is strong affection and intimacy between men and gods. The gods talk to their human protegés like Dutch uncles and even fight alongside them and suffer injury. When the gods are as close as that formal worship is not needed. But at other points in the narratives the gods are unseen, remote, forbidding and dangerous, and need to be propitiated by massive sacrifices.

I am not suggesting that these myths of the withdrawal of gods are historical. Their function is to show us what worship is now like by contrasting it with an imaginary earlier state of things. The myths express an ancient sense that the gods have become alien, problematic and of uncertain disposition. Men must signal to them in bold, urgent and unmistakable gestures if they hope to be heeded.

How are we to account for the formality of worship and the alienation between Gods and men? Naturally the Christian answer begins from the Fall-story, telling how in his pride and disobedience man sinned, and was justly punished by incurring exile from Paradise and perpetual sinfulness through generation after generation. However, redemption is on the way; there was a primal unity between God and man before the alienation-phase began and it will in the end be restored.

Even more significant, beneath this official top line of argument there is a somewhat different sub-plot which is also part of orthodox theology. The fall is a happy fault, *felix culpa*. What did our first parents desire? – the divine attributes, for they sought to be as gods, knowing good and evil (that is, everything), and God himself confirms that 'the man has become as one of us.' That the fall is in the long run a step upwards is confirmed by the fact that eventually redeemed man attains a higher dignity than unfallen man. After the period of alienation under the tutelage of the law is ended man becomes united with God through the immanent divine Spirit.

The atheist account of the part that the gods have played in the development of the human race is surprisingly similar to this traditional Christian one. The atheist also works with the same sequence of a primal unity followed by a time of alienation, leading to a restoration of unity at a higher level. For him too the formality of worship reflects the distance between what man now is and what he is yet to become. The primal unity is the dreaming innocence of the as-yet unconscious human subject, still immersed in nature. When man begins to become conscious a gap opens between what he is and what he should become. Belief in the gods expresses this sense of shortcoming, for the gods represent the freedom, spiritual autonomy and sovereignty over nature of which man obscurely knows he is capable but of which at the present time he falls so far short. The god is the future of man: what God is, man will become. The role of the god is precisely to lure man forward to the attainment of the god's own perfect self-possession and fully-achieved spiritual individuality. When that stage has been reached worship ceases because man now possesses and is what formerly he could only worship from afar.

It is striking how close the orthodox Christian and the atheist accounts are to each other. A famous passage from Kierkegaard's *The Sickness unto Death* has about it a truly remarkable ambiguity, of which he must have been aware. Kierkegaard was writing some years after the publication of Feuerbach's *Essence of Christianity*[5], a book that – if he read it – must surely have led him to wonder how far he was himself transforming traditional theism into something new and different. Kierkegaard has been saying that the fatalist who is imprisoned by natural necessity cannot pray, for he has no breath of freedom or possibility:

For in order to pray there must be a God, there must be a self

plus possibility, or a self and possibility in the pregnant sense;
for God *is* that all things are possible, and that all things are
possible *is* God; and only the man whose being has been so
shaken that he became spirit by understanding that all things
are possible, only he has had dealings with God. The fact that
God's will is the possible makes it possible for me to pray; if
God's will is only the necessary, man is essentially as speechless
as the brutes.[6]

Living after the Enlightenment and the Romantic Movement, Kierkegaard knows that the modern self is different from the self of
earlier epochs. The self in traditional society came to itself in
conforming itself to the given cosmic order. Its nature and destiny
were antecedently prescribed to it, and its task was simply to accept
them. The traditional self was a substance, with a given nature and
a given place in a ready-made scheme of things. By contrast, the
modern self is a process of becoming, a 'relation'.[7] It is self-defining, generating its own knowledge and its own destiny of becoming
a fully-achieved, conscious and autonomous spiritual subject. The
modern self must choose itself for itself, and Kierkegaard is attempting to Christianize this modern self. Indeed its vocation is to
become an existing individual subject which fully possesses itself
and wills to be itself, and God *is* that this is possible, both as
promise and demand. So Kierkegaard seeks to interpret in Christian
categories the modern task of becoming an individual, insisting
that the task is a terrifying and awesome one, much more difficult
than is usually supposed and such that only the Christian categories
can guide us through it. But in what he says he runs unnervingly
close to Feuerbach's account. He was correct, because the truth
does indeed lie close to Feuerbach; but how far did he realize it?

Both the Christian and the atheist emphasize the worshipper's
sense that he falls infinitely short of the object that he worships.
For the Christian, man worships as a sinner hoping for divine
mercy. For the atheist, worshipping man has not yet achieved full
maturity and autonomous individuality. His god is a projected
ideal, the self he has not yet become. When he does finally achieve
union with his god he becomes fully self-possessed and the age of
religion comes to an end. Thus for both the Christian and the
atheist religion is a temporary phenomenon. The Christian says
that there was no temple in paradise and there will be no temple
in the New Jerusalem (e.g. Rev. 21.22). The atheist says the fore-
runners of man had no gods and humanist man in the future will

need no gods, but during the long millenia in between the gods have done an important job in helping to develop human subjectivity. The gods presented an ideal of freedom and control over nature, power to order the world and so on, for man to aspire after. The gods were legislators until the time when man should internalize their legislative power and become fully self-legislating, ordering the world and his own moral life for himself. The genius of Hegel and Kierkegaard was that they attempted (albeit in opposed ways) to synthesize the two accounts and to show how religion might still be possible for the modern self.

Both had available to them the idea, deep in the biblical tradition, that there is no temple in the Heavenly City. The old law was written on tablets of stone. It was an objectified system of demands imposed upon man from outside with penal sanctions annexed. Man's only choice was the choice voluntarily to conform himself to a world-order and a moral order prescribed for him by an omnipotent will. This kind of religion is impossible to the modern self. But the Bible itself looks forward to, and in the New Testament has at least partly achieved, a new covenant in which the religious demand is fully internalized, being 'written on the heart', and objectification and alienation are overcome (e.g. Jer. 31.31ff.). In the old order the principles of human spiritual autonomy and of obedience to God contradicted each other, but the new covenant suggested that they might become identical. God's will for us is precisely that we should become fully-realized spiritual individuals through the overcoming of any distinction between him and us.

Hegel and Kierkegaard used these ideas in very different ways. Hegel saw the whole developing world-historical process as the embodiment of God, renamed *Geist* or Spirit. History is the evolution of Spirit towards full self-realization. But there is not any God over and above human subjectivities, except in the sense that the whole is greater than the parts and the future greater than the present. God is as it were the soul of history. Kierkegaard rejected this global religiosity, focussed his thought upon the individual's task of becoming a subject, and retains much more of the traditional language of divine transcendence; though it must be noted that in his thought God's transcendence is not metaphysical but intensely religious and internalized. To go back to the distinction from which we began, he is an expressivist rather than a realist. For him the transcendence of God cannot be anything other than the unconditional authority of the religious demand that I become a fully-realized spiritual subject.

What was it that had happened to belief in God at the beginning of the nineteenth century? It seemed to the leading thinkers that an old kind of throne-and-altar religion had died. Man could no longer see himself as the subject of an absolute monarch, a metaphysically transcendent creator and ruler of the cosmos who was to be worshipped by a kind of extension of court ritual. Human morality, knowledge and destiny were increasingly seen not as passively accepted from on high but as actively generated from within man himself. Kierkegaard's response was radically to internalize the religious demand. He shows little or no interest in the objective or cosmological side of religion. His God speaks only to and within the self about what the self must become.

What Kierkegaard did for religion resembles what Kant had done for morality. Kant utterly rejected any derivation of the authority of morality from nature. The authority of morality in no way depends upon questions of fact, technique or consequences. It is rather recognized inwardly by practical reason as autonomous and unconditionally authoritative. Similarly, for Kierkegaard the religious demand is not something inferred from facts about the external world. It establishes itself autonomously and inwardly within the self as an inescapable claim upon the self.

What then becomes of the objectivity of worship? Surely, people will say, worship is undeniably addressed to one other than the worshippers, a King of the universe who makes all things, knows all things and rules all things? Worship is directed towards a cosmos-transcending absolute being, and those who deny that there is any such being are atheists.

We have sketched a series of objections to this naive realism. Worship does not actually postulate that the god is present in just the same way as a king giving audience is present to the petitioners. Secondly, though it is true that worship has a very complex dramatic character, its elaborate formality is really an expression of the distance and mysteriousness of the god. And thirdly, what is the meaning of this distance? Here we came to the intriguing point that Christian and atheist are agreed in essentials about what is happening. Both say that in worship we postulate an ideal of spiritual autonomy and sovereignty of which we are conscious of falling far short, but with which we long to be united. Thus the basic language and aspirations of worship are quite capable of an expressivist and ideal interpretation. Although the externals of worship may suggest an objectified courtly service, believers know that it is a mistake to remain stuck at that level of understanding.

For what really matters is something very different, namely the secret and subjective claim that is made upon the inwardness of the worshipper. And here God is precisely not objective, but internal to 'the heart'.

So much is this true that there are powerful objections to the realistic view of worship and its object. It cannot be proved – and is quite implausible to suppose – that the cosmos resembles a state ruled by an all-wise and all-powerful monarch, and even if there were such a being it is not clear how he could create the unconditional and inward authority of the religious demand. On the contrary, one might, like Kant, object to the worship of such a being, for the traditional arguments against a heteronomous morality are applicable also to heteronomous worship. Moral principles prescribed to me by a very powerful and authoritative being who backs them up with threat and promise are not truly moral, for my moral principles – if they are to be truly moral – must be freely acknowledged by me as intrinsically authoritative and freely adopted as my own. Indeed I must in a profound way identify my very being with the morality I profess. Many people suppose that it somehow helps the objectivity of morals that there should be an objective ground and ordainer of the moral, but the truth is the opposite. The more objectively the-moral-standard-as-the-will-of-God be conceived, the more it destroys morality. Morality has to have its own proper kind of disinterestedness, which means that it cannot accept the support of external guarantees and sanctions. Sanctions may have a transitional and educational part to play and they may have a useful function as picturesque mythological reinforcements. In this way imagery of heavenly rewards and hellish punishments may usefully remind me of the importance of moral choice from moment to moment. But if I make the mistake of supposing that heaven and hell exist and allow fear and hope to determine my conduct, I am ceasing to be moral.

So, finally, there is a persuasive *religious* argument against a realistic view of worship, namely that the more realistically or objectively we conceive God and worship the more we run into the paradoxes of religious objectification.

These paradoxes are much more severe than people realize. They are all grouped around the idea of religious disinterestedness. For it would be generally agreed that the mark of a truly religious character is that it displays a certain detachment, disinterestedness, egolessness, non-defensiveness, non-acquisitiveness, simplicity and absence of any drive to self-justification. But if to be truly religious is to be disinterested in this way, then religious concern must be non-objective. For if religion is supposed to consist in an interest in possessing or attaining various external objects such as a realistically-understood God and life after death, then it is precisely *not* disinterested.

Kierkegaard makes the point very eloquently when he commends the remembrance of the dead as a pre-eminent example of disinterested love.[8] The dead do not change, cannot respond, and are not there any more. If we love them it cannot be in the hope of any reciprocation; our love must be truly disinterested. D. Z. Phillips argues that because a truly religious spirit must be quite disinterested it cannot expect to be rewarded after death.[9] The only fitting reward for religious disinterestedness must be non-objective or internal, in the sense that (as people rightly say) it is 'its own reward'.

Similarly, what is disinterested love? Love is desire, so how can it be disinterested? The answer must surely be that love is pure and disinterested when it is expressive and non-objective so that its object (God) is internal to it. When one loves in that way then one is in the love of God. Possessive pronouns and the subject-object distinction cease to be important, and sacred love can equally well be described as my love for God or as God's love for me. As so many writers have hinted, there is a blessed ambiguity between the subjective and objective genitive in the phrase, 'the love of God'. Just as in the sphere of morality I must identify my very being with the morality I profess, so in religious worship I must identify my very being with what I worship. In religion there is no independent being whose existence validates the practice of worship, just as in morality there is no independent being whose will validates the principles of morality. There does not need to be such an independent being, for the aim of worship is to declare one's complete and *disinterested* commitment to religious values. Belief in the God of Christian faith is an expression of allegiance to a particular set of values, and experience of the God of Christian faith is experience of the impact of those values in one's life.

6

DOCTRINE AND DISINTERESTEDNESS

Words like 'realism' and 'objectivity' have such reassuring over-tones of sobriety and old-fashioned virtue that it is easy to be deceived by them. We can be led carelessly to imagine that realist doctrines have about them an honesty and straightforwardness that almost guarantees their intelligibility and makes any close scrutiny of them superfluous. Certainly in relation to Christian doctrines there is no doubt that most people, believers or not, begin with a very strong presumption that realist accounts make sense and have right on their side.

Yet in every single case the more closely we examine these realist accounts the more perplexing they become, and I for one confess that I have never understood any of them. In some cases I cannot even begin to guess what a realist account of the doctrine might be: what, for instance, is the realist interpretation of the doctrine that forty days after Easter Jesus 'ascended into Heaven and is seated at the right hand of God'? In other cases there are problems of consistency. Thus, objective theories of the atoning death of Christ are traditionally assumed to have more religious weight in them than subjective theories. But those who put forward objective theories of the atonement also put forward objective or realist views about God with the result that they seem to contradict themselves, for under the first heading they must claim that Christ's death somehow marks a change in God while under the latter heading they must say that God is unchangeable. Objectivism about the atonement seems to be incompatible with various trad-itional beliefs about God.

Though we have discussed it already, the resurrection of Jesus has to be mentioned again here for it is the most vivid example of the strength of the presumption in favour of realism. Everybody is so very sure that he knows just what it is and that the realist account is obviously correct. Yet on reflection we find that the realist account is plainly incoherent. For what is it that the apostles claimed to have seen? The realist says they claimed to have seen with their own eyes the very same Jesus, alive again and in the very same body. So far, perfectly clear; but if that is what the apostles claim, then by the same token they are also claiming that what they saw was something alive but with a life that was no longer biological, for it had died and was now immortal; something which did not need to eat yet might do so; something which, although a physical object, could appear and disappear and pass through walls; something which has since become invisible and ubiquitous, having passed beyond time and change, while yet appearing on altars and so forth; and this thing of which all those statements are true is still the very same human body of the very same Jesus of Nazareth. So says the realist, and I say this is incomprehensible. What, for example, is it for a human body to be alive with a non-biological life? We have no idea. Yet the realist will not admit any difficulty and remains convinced that he is on firm ground and cannot be dislodged.

In the case of God we find a similar very strong but unexamined bias towards a realist account, and here again the realist view turns out to be harder to maintain than people think. So long as we remain in the areas of worship, prayer, the spiritual life and the indwelling of God within the human soul then talk of God is not too difficult, for it need not be understood as making transcendent metaphysical claims. But when we move to the metaphysical, the cosmological and the objective side of theism (the only aspect of theism that most philosophers consider) then we run into problems.

In relation to the proofs of God, I have already argued that we do not seem to be in possession of a valid proof of the existence of the realist's God. I have also suggested that even if one day one of the proofs should be stated in a form that commanded general acceptance (an unlikely event, it must be admitted) it would still not necessarily do all that much for theological realism. To recall just one key point, in classical European times and in India much the same arguments were adduced in support of doctrines quite different from realistic monotheism. The argument from design has been advanced in the cause of pantheism.[1] So even if in some form or other it should turn out to be valid, what would it prove? We are not entitled to be sure that it would prove the existence of the God of the realists.

Now we add the further point that we do not know for sure whether theistic realism is even coherent. The issue is sharply debated among contemporary philosophers, who pose the question in such terms as these:

Can there be a mind that is not embodied?

How can we think of a bodiless mind as active at every point in the universe? We are told not to think of God as animating the world in the way the human mind animates the human body, but if God's relation to nature is not like that then what is it like? We seem to have no analogies to help us to understand it.

If there is an infinite mind with complete knowledge of the future, then surely determinism is true? But determinism seems incompatible with other things theists say about God in his relation to the world and men.

If there is an infinite mind with all knowledge and power, then it is surely responsible for evil?

If such a mind is to know all that happens in an ever-changing universe, how can it be immutable?

Can there in any case *be* an immutable mind? A person who does not change is surely not alive?

Among contemporary philosophers some think that a coherent – or at any rate, possibly coherent and not demonstrably incoherent – realist doctrine of God can be framed.[2] Others say not.[3] But the current debates about coherence are in my opinion of limited usefulness. Philosophers have become involved with them because they think it is not their business to settle questions of fact, and so they must chastely restrict themselves to more formal questions about what is and is not conceivable; questions about, not what *is* so, but what must be so, what may conceivably be so, and what cannot possibly be so. This 'logicism' is an appropriate method for subjects like mathematics, where meanings are clear, fixed invariable things, very precisely analysable, but in such areas as religion, morality, art and politics meanings are plainly not like that. On the contrary, they are inevitably very imprecise and different for different people and at different periods. Take the question, 'Can there be a disembodied mind?' In an animistic culture people will tend to answer Yes, but in a culture in which explanation has become predominantly mechanistic they will tend to answer, No. To ignore this fact and try to answer the question by abstract and unhistorical conceptual analysis is rather unprofitable.

Earlier philosophy raised other and in some ways more searching questions. For example: the highest branch of philosophy is ethics, for philosophy's chief task is to show the way to eternal blessedness. God is by definition that the contemplation and enjoyment of which is eternal blessedness. So philosophy must attain to supremely lucid rational contemplation of God. That is philosophy's mission and goal. Yet we are told that the God of orthodox monotheism is a free, transcendent and ultimately incomprehensible will, a God who is not perfectly knowable but who on the contrary confronts us with an ultimate dualism and a mystery that cannot be overcome. This is a contradiction. Such a being cannot be the true God who is the goal of the philosopher's quest. The objective monotheist's account of God is therefore severely criticized by philosophy. It needs drastic revision – perhaps of the sort that Spinoza carried out so impressively.

Again, theists say there is an actual infinite divine substance, as it were over and above and distinct from this world about us of changing finite things. But am I saying anything that I can understand, when I speak of something 'beyond' the world altogether? Within the world of experience I can speak of one thing as greater than another, as lying beyond another, as explaining another, as transcending (or surpassing) another and as causing another. But all those five relations are relations that normally hold between two things both of which are within the world of experience. While we stay within the bounds of experience we can spell out just what we mean. But it is something else again to claim that there can be a relation of the same kind between the world as a whole and some world-transcending thing. How can I tell in such a case whether what I say means anything or not? I do not want to fall into the logicism of trying to demonstrate by pure conceptual analysis either that talk of a transcendent being is meaningful or that it is meaningless. I am just saying that I do not know which it is – or how to find out.

Alternatively, suppose I start from the other end of the problem. Like Parmenides and other monists I become convinced that the only contradiction-free account of reality as a whole is that which represents it as one eternal and infinite substance. But if so, how can there 'also' exist a world of many finite beings 'alongside' the infinite? If reality is one infinite divine substance then surely it fills all and there is no space for anything else to be?

To meet the difficulty it is sometimes said that God, being infinite in power, must also have the power to budge over a bit and limit himself so as to make room for a created world to exist as well as himself. In creating a world the Infinite graciously restricts or veils itself a little. There is a divine *kenosis* in creation.

So it is said, but we do not know if we talk sense when we say such a thing, and the feeling that paradoxes are approaching suggests that we may be talking nonsense. For the claim that the omnipotent can limit himself reminds us of the various traditional paradoxes of omnipotence. These paradoxes are questions which, whether answered yes or no, seem to give rise to a contradiction. Thus, to start with a simple conundrum, 'Can the Pope infallibly pronounce himself to be fallible after all?' Now one about God: 'Can God set himself a problem that he cannot solve?' And the case presently in question: 'Has God, being omnipotent, the power to renounce some part of his own powers and so become, in that particular respect, no longer omnipotent?'

I do not pretend that these questions are very profitable to consider. I suggest only that it is reasonable to suspect when paradoxes like these loom near that there may be nonsense about. Perhaps the reason why a realist or literalist account of the meaning of infallibility gives rise to paradoxes is that there is something wrong with the idea, and the same may be true of the realist notion of divine omnipotence.

It seems that we can hardly avoid being triply agnostic about the realist view of God. It is not certain that his existence can be proved, it is not certain whether or not the idea of such a being is even coherent, and, as I have already argued in earlier chapters, it is not certain that theological realism is such a good thing anyway. Alternatives to it would seem to be possible, in spite of the hostility that many people feel towards theological revision. For it is an obvious historical fact that concepts, and also entire belief-systems, do undergo profound transformations and revisions in the course of time. Hegel saw this, and he helped to introduce a new kind of philosophical argument – much used in this book – in which one takes up a particular set of meanings and beliefs and by pressing their own inner logic transforms them into something significantly new and different.

In all religious traditions theologians have always done this, because it is their peculiar duty to preserve a tradition by changing it. It must be changed if it is to survive, but it has not survived unless the inner spiritual continuity between the old pattern and the new is so persuasively argued that the constituency can with a clear conscience move over to the new standpoint.

History lays upon the Christian theologian the duty radically to transform Christianity and by so doing to preserve its identity. Nineteenth-century philosophy, after Hegel, made us much more aware than people had been in earlier times of just how the trick is done. Unhappily, modern Anglo-Saxon philosophy is quite un-historically-minded and so does not understand why theological conservation necessitates drastic theological revision.

In a recent book, Dr Anthony Kenny neatly though unconscious-ly exemplifies both the prejudice against and the possibility of theological revision. He sniffs at the way 'Church leaders hasten to abandon those parts of their message which make it distinguish-able from the current fashion in secular reasoning,'[4] and yet in the very same chapter he raises this interesting 'question in the spirit of Kierkegaard: "Suppose that the philosophical difficulties about the attributes of God were all cleared up: suppose that the Five Ways, or the ontological argument, were shown to be valid – would it then be any more reasonable than now to give the absolute commitment?" '[5] And Kenny answers, No. Surely, he says, no philosophical position can be so secure that it is reasonable to commit one's whole way of life upon it.

Kenny does not pursue the question he has raised. He remains a realist. He wishes that belief in God could be defended philo-sophically, because he thinks theism needs a philosophical basis – even though unfortunately we don't seem able to construct one for it. But since Kenny himself holds that objective theism appears to be unprovable and incoherent and that in any case it cannot make us religious – i.e., commit our whole lives – why is he still so attached to realism? Where is the sense in clinging so hard to a view of God which he has just shown to be nonsense? In the analogous case of platonic universals, once we have acknowledged that there are not any real universals what we do is formulate an alternative to the realist account. We should do the same in the case of God.

For mark well this further point of analogy between the two cases: One reason for dropping the realist account of universals is that, so conceived, they do not do very well at solving the problems of meaning they were postulated to solve. Similarly, the realist account of God does not do very well at solving the problem it is postulated to solve, namely the justification of religious commitment's unique intensity. For suppose that there are such things as metaphysical facts, and that God's existence is one of them – what can such facts do to make us unconditionally religious? The parallel with ethics is obvious. It has long been widely agreed that you cannot validly deduce statements about what ought to be done from statements merely about matters of fact, even metaphysical fact. The case for the autonomy of religion is parallel, but is if anything even stronger because religious commitment is so much greater and more demanding than moral commitment. In morality one can, as it were, occasionally relax. One is allowed to take a break and indeed it is prudent to do so – I do not mean by acting immorally, but simply by relaxing the ordinary strenuousness and punctiliousness of moral endeavour. Sometimes it is right to take it easy. In religion there is no such possibility, for religious commitment is day and night, sleeping and waking; it is one's entire mode of being and there cannot be a holiday from it. Secondly, much, much more than morality, religion is a requirement of absolute disinterestedness, and that one should be thus absolutely disinterested is not a thing that can be determined *ab extra* by any metaphysical fact whatever. Morality is a matter of acts, habits of action and dispositions and it is social. We have periods of perfectly legitimate inaction, and occasions when we quite rightly act for our own good. But religion is a matter of our whole existence, of our commitment to existence and of absolute disinterestedness in our relation to our own existence. It is not a consequential matter at all. Nothing outside me can make it advisable for me to start being religious, because religiousness is quite beyond considerations of either prudence or clockwatching. You cannot drop out of religion *for a time*, because in so far as one is religious one is not in time nor subject to it. The religious is timeless and disinterested. It is the highest degree of dispassionate compassion, selfless self-awareness, and *disponibilité* or attentive and free availability to others. In this state we are in the love of God, and its autonomy expresses the divine aseity. That is what it is to be religious, and it is different from morality. Morality has been plausibly represented by great moralists as largely or wholly determined by considerations of reasonable and cool self-love or of utility, but you could not possibly say such things about religion; so that if there is nevertheless a respectable case for the autonomy of ethics, then there is a much stronger case for the autonomy of religion.

What of the objection that the drift of the whole argument is towards a complete severance between religious existence and objective doctrinal claim? Surely, it will be said, people have in the past lived their religious lives within the comfortable and supportive frameworks of rich and complex doctrinal belief-systems. If our argument is sound, there is not a deductive relationship between doctrinal claim and religious obligation because the supposition that there is leads to intolerable paradoxes. For example, it would be very paradoxical for God to say, 'Love me for my goodness with a pure disinterested love or I'll see you roast in hell!' So when religious doctrines are propounded in order to encourage us to religious commitment, we had better say that they operate in an informal and mythological fashion. They are not reasons but merely illustrations. We are told that certain moral principles are God's revealed will, that God is coming in judgment, and that he will reward the pure in heart, and when we are told these things we are told them in order to kindle our imaginations and incite us to be religious. The doctrines work not as rational motives but merely as picturesque reinforcements of the autonomous religious requirement; and in order to prevent them from doing any harm they are supplemented by other teaching which emphasizes that religious dispositions must be truly disinterested.

So it may be argued that, as in the past, so in the future religious existence will continue for most people to be commended and imaginatively supported by a rich doctrinal belief-system. There is no problem; it is easy to build in safeguards so that people understand the point about disinterestedness. To defend doctrinal objectivism, the Council of Trent said that it was perfectly correct for the Christian to be motivated by the thought of heavenly rewards and hellish punishments.[6] But a writer of the same communion also says:

> My God, I love thee, not because
> I hope for heaven thereby,
> Nor yet because who love thee not
> Are lost eternally.

And we must suppose that all proficient believers are well aware that disinterested love is the higher value.

This defence of objective theological doctrines as picturesque reinforcers and as imaginative stimulants is itself fairly sceptical — as indeed it has to be. For not only is there the problem that if doctrine be taken too literally it destroys religion but there is also the familiar problem of the diversity of belief-systems. Truly religious people can crop up, and can have a good deal in common with each other so far as religiousness or piety is concerned, in doctrinally very diverse settings.[7] Surely doctrine cannot matter so very much? In our new global culture local religious ideologies are unlikely ever again quite to recover their former standing, for it is so obvious that they are merely local and not universal.

This is not a congenial admission to have to make. In the seventeenth and eighteenth centuries people tried very hard to fend it off. They struggled to establish by philosophical argument that there was a truly universal and cross-cultural natural theology, and they tried to verify empirically the existence of a correspondingly universal natural religion. They were right to be so worried, for it is a very serious matter to be obliged to conclude that whereas there is truly universal scientific knowledge, there is not any universal and cross-cultural religious knowledge at all. But by now we have been forced to that admission, and in addition it would seem from my general characterization of it that a truly and fully religious existence is possible that does not presuppose any metaphysical claims. Nor need any metaphysical inferences be drawn from it, as we shall see. They *may* be drawn, but they do not *need* to be drawn.

It is worth emphasizing that what we have said by no means tends towards the elimination of *all* religious doctrine. For it is clearly part of religious doctrine to characterize religious existence, to summon people to it, and to commend it with stories about saints and martyrs and by the reading of scriptures. Nor am I suggesting that talk of God and the lived relation of God will be cut out. Far from it. But God will be spoken of roughly as people speak of the pearl of great price – that is, not in a cosmological or metaphysical way, but in the context of the spiritual life and as that about which the spiritual life revolves. The element of doctrine which will be drastically 'demythologized' is the part which appears to make metaphysical claims about a supernatural world, about supernatural beings and about supernatural causes of events. We do not have sufficient reason for believing in any such supernatural world or being or cause, and it is open to question whether talk of such things makes any sense at all. It certainly seems not to make sense under modern intellectual conditions. But one can be truly religious in the highest degree without being committed to belief in such things.

In the course of the argument I have been agnostic about supernatural beings and causes, rather than denying them outright. This lays me open to another possible retort by the realist. 'What you are doing', he says, 'is trying to retain religious values in an age when – as you suppose – religious beliefs have died. But you are agnostic and surely on your own showing supernaturalist beliefs, though they cannot be proved, cannot be conclusively disproved either. Is not faith therefore just as much entitled to its own point of view as is unfaith? William James was correct: we have a right to believe where belief is life-enhancing, and the believer's point of view is neither more nor less rational than anyone else's.'

I do not think this appeal for permissiveness is acceptable. Gratuitous overbeliefs are not neutral things. They are often very harmful, and it would be better to discipline the mind to economy and spareness. Furthermore, in real life it would often be preferable to have rather more human moral effort and rather less daydreaming about supernatural agencies.

There are other things that people say to themselves by way of encouraging themselves to cling on to supernaturalist beliefs. They may say, for example, that they accept the doctrines for the sake of the precious values associated with them. But I have argued that the religious values are in the end autonomous and do not need such support. Besides, it often happens that the traditionally-associated doctrines do as much to threaten as to support religious values – as, for example, when belief in heaven and hell does something to make me try to be religious, but only at the price of threatening the supremely important quality of religious disinterestedness and purity of heart.

A protest against subjectivist and internalizing tendencies in modern religious thought is made very forcibly by Professor Donald MacKinnon.[8] He thinks that the internalizers are withdrawing from engagement with the world of empirical fact. Formerly, the doctrines of the incarnation, the resurrection, divine providence and so forth obliged the believer to make claims about and so to involve himself with real history. But nowadays these grand old doctrines are increasingly being reinterpreted in subjectivist ways. Faith deserts the world of politics and economics and withdraws into the inner life. Clerical pietism replaces the old concern for social action.

In reply I say that if this happens it is certainly deplorable, but there is no reason for it to happen. On the contrary, in at least some classic cases the internalization of religious concepts had the effect of shifting the domain of their application away from the

makes a good case

narrowly religious sphere to that of social ethics. The classic case is the transformation by the Israelite prophets of the concept of holiness. The holy was originally specifically religious and not at all ethical. Like high-voltage electrification, it was the charge of sacred and dangerous power which protected religious objects from profanation by the impious. But the prophets gradually changed the meaning of holiness. As belonging to God, Israel was itself seen as holy in a way that required appropriate ethical expression. Eventually holiness became almost the same as righteousness:

> ... the LORD of hosts is exalted in justice,
> and the Holy God shows himself holy in righteousness.
> > (Isa. 5.16)

Holiness was at first objective. It was seen as an empirical property of certain specific objects, places and so on in the external world. The prophets reinterpreted it, shifting both the criteria for applying the term and the domain in which it was applied, so that it became a moral quality of persons. Holiness as a religiously-significant quality ceases to be an objective feature of certain external objects, and is internalized and moralized. Yet the outcome is not a retreat from social ethics, but a movement into it. MacKinnon's criticism seems to be unfair. When we reinterpret religious doctrines in a subjective or internalized way and come to see religious values as autonomously authoritative it does not at all follow that we are likely to retreat into private pietism. Kant carried out a similar internalization of morality, but he did not therefore lose interest in politics and international relations.

Others will argue: 'I recognize the autonomous authority and the bindingness of religious values, and I accept the supernatural doctrines as transcendental presuppositions of the bindingness of the values.' That is something of a mouthful: what I mean is this – I know prayer is intrinsically worthwhile so I will suppose there is someone to pray to; I know that the sense of life as a pilgrimage is intrinsically valuable so I will suppose that there is a goal of life to which we will come after death; and I know it is intrinsically good to be humble so I will suppose there is one to be humble before, one from whom I receive every good thing. At least some religious doctrines might in this way be called (still borrowing Kantian jargon) religious postulates. In my religious existence I find myself acting as if those things were true which appear to be presupposed by the intrinsically valuable religious practices that I have adopted. In that sense, I do believe many traditional doctrines.

The obvious reply is the Buddhist one, that such postulates involve no real religious gain and some loss. For the Buddhist will say that it is better to treat life as a pilgrimage towards nirvana than to treat it as a pilgrimage towards everlasting life in another and heavenly world, that meditation is better than dialogue prayer, and that self-reliance on the path to salvation is better than dependency. These Buddhist retorts suggest that autonomous and purely disinterested religious values are the best and the most nearly universal, for as soon as we begin to see our religious values in relation to some particular local doctrinal system we lose something of universality and something of disinterestedness, and begin to introduce local cultural distortions. ⟶ I don't believe it is possible to avoid such a happe thing i.e. Jelesten Bule - Maybe

Let us give the theological realist one more reply. Let him say that it is foolish of me to talk as if I can transcend the limitations of my own religious and cultural heritage and be religious in a truly universal way. There is no 'natural' or universal religiousness; there are only the particular, 'positive' and regional traditions. My attempt at transcendence will lead merely to impoverishment and perhaps emptiness. At the very least one must – with a touch of ironic detachment, no doubt – be loyal to one's own religious and cultural tradition.

Such loyalty is inescapable (the realist continues), for the only cross-culturally universal objective knowledge that we have is scientific knowledge, and that is not enough to live by. Where matters of culture and mores are concerned there is no option but an ironical, tolerant and non-exclusive allegiance to one's own tradition.

Yes, indeed: but what has just been stated is neither more nor less than traditional sceptical teaching. It is not realism but scepticism that is here being advocated, which reminds us of just how sceptical are most of the arguments that are nowadays produced to justify allegiance to received doctrines. And there is a difficulty, for in Montaigne's day there was still one prevailing popular religion to which the prudent sceptic politely conformed. Today most of that has gone and there are only a few rites – weddings, funerals, Christmas, memorial services – which are still socially almost obligatory, and which people attend in the authentic spirit of sceptical respect and courtesy on the ground that these are the established and decent customs of society. Outside that very small area there is today a vast range of options and little real social pressure upon adults to conform to any of them. So the traditional sceptical argument for religious conformity – that it is proper to take part in the local rites and beliefs, for they are neither more nor less valid than any other similar decent observances – has much less force nowadays. On the contrary, one might well ask instead the searching question, What is wrong with Christian Buddhism?

I mean this: to put it bluntly, we are and have been for many generations in a position where not one single religious doctrine (of the sort that mentions supernatural beings, events and causes) can be established by a reputable intellectual method. Not one. Yet it is also the case that there are many obviously admirable and beautiful religious attitudes, values, practices and so forth which ought not to pass away altogether. Here are some of them:

> It is good that one should appraise oneself and one's life with an unconditional religious seriousness that tolerates no concealment or self-deception.

> It is good that one should cultivate meditation and contemplative prayer, and especially the inner fortitude and resilience needed to combat evils of all kinds.

> It is good that one should come to transcend the mean defensive ego and learn absolute disinterestedness and purity of heart.

> It is good that one should commit oneself to existence in religious hope and receptivity to grace.

> In spite of all the ugliness and cruelty in the world, it is good that one should at least sometimes experience and express cosmic awe, thanksgiving and love.

> It is good that such values as these should not only be cultivated in and for oneself, but that they should shape our attitudes towards other people and be expressed in our social life.

That is part at least of what I mean by 'religious values', and I specify them only because people so often refer in passing to religious values without pausing to say what they might be. So I suggest that the six values just described are precious things and if possible ought not to be lost from human life.

Now imagine a person who is sceptical or at any rate agnostic about all the metaphysical and doctrinal aspects of traditional Christian belief but who very much wishes to cultivate the ethics, the inwardness, the spirituality and many of the ritual practices of Christianity. He speaks of God, but he speaks of God as within the soul, talking of God rather as mystics of many faiths speak of a jewel, diamond or pearl; that is, as that infinitely-precious indescribable secret which is the goal of the spiritual life and about which the spiritual life revolves. That, he thinks, is the best way to speak of God. Furthermore, our Christian Buddhist speaks also of Jesus, but he does not think of Jesus as the divine Christ of the church who lives and reigns in a higher world, because he has no reason to think there is any such higher world. Instead he studies the tradition of the words of that neglected spiritual master, the historical Jesus. Finally, suppose that he makes such progress in the religious life as to become obviously and identifiably a deeply religious and even saintly person. Yet so far as doctrinal orthodoxy is concerned he scores zero, as he freely admits.

Just what would be wrong with such a position? A traditional believer who attaches importance to creeds and orthodoxy would doubtless feel very threatened by our Christian Buddhist and would express disapproval. But if he is really to defend orthodoxy, he must give some reason why non-doctrinal religiousness is unsatisfactory. It is all the more necessary to do so because the Christian Buddhist has one very strong point in his favour: he is much closer to people of other faiths than is his doctrine-affirming critic. His religion may not be fully universal but at least it is a great deal less parochial than the other's.

7

THE MEANING OF GOD

So what is wrong with the position I have just described as Christian Buddhism? Not much. It shows intellectual virtue in refraining from making unnecessary and unprovable doctrinal claims. But it is incomplete, and I shall certainly be expected to provide a much more detailed and clearer explanation of what 'God' is and the part God plays in the spiritual life than has yet been given. People do feel dissatisfied and cheated when presented with anything other than the metaphysical view of God that comes ultimately from Philo of Alexandria, who lived from about 20 BC to AD 50. Nevertheless, as we have seen, there are various reasons for trying to break with this realist or metaphysical view of God. It seems that we do not have sufficiently good grounds for thinking that such a being exists, there are some doubts about whether he even *can* exist, he threatens human spiritual and moral autonomy, he threatens the principle of the autonomy of religion, and in any case scripture – the teaching of men like the prophets and Jesus – is pre-philosophical and is by no means unambiguously committed to any one particular view as to the kind of reality that God has. It is sometimes forgotten by philosophers who denounce anti-metaphysical theologies that people contrived to believe in God before the God of the philosophers was invented, people who were quite innocent of platonism or any other species of metaphysics. So maybe some alternative to the realist view of God is possible, and maybe behind the philosophical ways of thinking about God there are more archaic religious ways which can help us in the task of grasping the post-metaphysical meaning of God.

The new religious meaning of God will however not be the same as the old, even though it will learn from it. We said earlier that the original prophetic type of experience of God is today no longer available to us. The modern concern for the autonomy of the individual human spirit, and the closely-related concern for the autonomy of purely religious values and claims, make it no longer possible for us to have quite the original prophetic experience of being summoned by an alien almighty and commanding will. The awesome theophany of pure commanding authority seems not to occur now. For us God is no longer a distinct person over against us who authoritatively and by his *ipse dixit* imposes the religious demand upon us. If he did so present himself we would have to reject him. The moral law similarly no longer depends, and cannot depend, upon a divine command for its authority. We recognize it as autonomously authoritative and freely choose to impose it upon ourselves. That is what it is, nowadays, to be a moral agent. Similarly, the religious requirement, that we must become spirit, is no longer now laid upon us by another but is autonomously authoritative. God is not an almighty individual other than the religious requirement whose will creates the religious requirement, makes it authoritative and binds it upon us. Rather, God *is* the religious requirement personified, and his attributes are a kind of projection of its main features as we experience them.

For example, to be religious means that one's whole life is as it were subject to a constant scrutiny and under assessment from an absolute point of view that silently records everything and misses nothing. The religious requirement extends to one's whole life and to every detail of one's life. It does not allow one to keep any secret compartments or locked doors. It searches the heart. And it is of course this feature of the religious demand that has given rise to the traditional affirmation of the omniscience of God.

In metaphysical theology the divine omniscience is understood as if there were a super-intelligence of infinite capacity, its memory stocked with all true propositions: 'The doctrine of omniscience is easy to formulate precisely: it is the doctrine that, for all p, if p, then God knows that p.'[1] But the same writer who so defines God's omniscience is also obliged to admit that this infinite memory-bank (an utterly non-religious idea, obviously) is not God's omniscience as described in the Bible: 'The Old and New Testament passages describing God's omniscience are too poetical and rhetorical for it to be possible to decide how literally their writers intended the idea that God knows everything.'[2]

This still misses the point. The Bible is inexact metaphysics because it is quite unconcerned with metaphysics, but as religion there is nothing wrong with it, for it is always very clear and precise. It makes two points about God's knowledge. First, biblical knowledge is always intensely practical and ethical; it is knowledge of good and evil and knowledge of what to do. God is not interested in accumulating information for its own sake. God's business is with sifting, discerning, weighing in the balance, searching out and discriminating, because God is judge, and judges have to know the whole truth in order to pass just judgment. God is only interested in religiously-relevant knowledge, not knowledge in general. So secondly, God's knowledge is always, and above all, knowledge of mysteries and secrets. It is always knowledge of things men do not know, do not want to know, do not want to become publicly known, or do not yet know.

We can grasp the point here if we ask ourselves why the Bible never represents God as knowing what everybody knows, or what is manifestly and publicly obvious. Why is God interested only in what is hidden? To a theological realist this must surely convey a rather quaint impression of a snooper or busybody; but no, that is not the point. The point is that the religious requirement is for complete spiritual integrity, for purity of heart and for an entire change of life. Nothing can be kept secret or withheld from it. It is precisely what I have most carefully hidden and have kept most deeply buried that the religious requirement insists on bringing to light. I do not begin to be truly religious until I have faced things that I have hidden even from myself and quite forgotten; and in that sense the religious requirement seems to be omniscient, for it searches the heart and knows me better than I know myself. It breaks down barriers to self-knowledge that I have erected as internal defences within myself. For what the religious requirement exposes and brings to light is always bad news. Hence it is spoken of as judging us and condemning us.

How does this happen? I am capable of being religious and recognizing the authority of the religious requirement insofar as I have attained some modest degree of self-awareness. The natural man's self-awareness, self-criticism and self-mastery are very imperfect indeed, but even such as they are they give him some small measure of transcendence of his fate. He is no longer merely as one of the beasts that perish. He can begin to think himself and his relation to his own existence, and this very modest power to know, criticize and change himself enables him to recognize the religious requirement as demanding and promising a complete and final knowledge, criticism and transformation of himself through which alone he can attain complete emancipation from fate – in a word, salvation. But the modest measure of self-knowledge that he has already got has been deeply influenced by his wishes. It is highly selective and, worse than that, distorted. It is a kind of idealized, propagandist and self-deceiving self-image, a false ego with a good deal of wounded vanity, resentment, fear and so on built into it. Into my natural self-understanding I build, for example, a theory of why it is that other people do not yet recognize my merits as they ought to do.

Given all this, which is disagreeably familiar and upon which it would be superfluous to dwell at present, the religious requirement must be experienced as condemnation before it can be experienced as salvation; it has to take us apart before it can remake us. So I have as it were to cast myself upon its mercy. Is this a reprehensible surrender of autonomy, a case of grovelling before something on no better grounds than that it is bigger, more knowledgeable and more powerful than I am? No, for the religious requirement is not an objectively-existing individual being quite distinct from myself. It is a judgment upon myself and a way to salvation that I have freely invoked upon myself and for myself. In one of its more demythologizing moments, the Fourth Gospel itself recognizes that we bring judgment upon ourselves. That is true, and more so than most people think.

The religious requirement is not heteronomy, in the sense of being an odious subjection to the will of another such as is incompatible with the dignity of a conscious rational self. It is true that I cast myself on God's mercy, knowing that the false self I have made of myself must die before I can attain my spiritual destiny. But I do not suppose God to be an objective individual over and above the religious requirement. The religious requirement has been radically internalized and made my own, so that *I* will its judgment upon myself.

But if the religious requirement is not heteronomy, neither is it a way of vulgar self-affirmation. On the contrary, it is the way of the cross and demands the surrender of everything. It is true that I know I can achieve my spiritual destiny just because I am *capax dei*, that is, capable of recognizing and laying upon myself the religious demand. But there is no vulgar self-affirmation here, for my spiritual destiny is precisely to achieve perfect disinterestedness, and a kind of selfhood so different from my present natural ego that by present standards it seems almost like egolessness, for it is perfectly non-acquisitive, non-defensive, self-communicating and free. Such a spiritual objective is neither heteronomous nor vulgarly egoistic and man-centred.

And God is not only the requirement personified, but also the goal personified. When we choose God we choose a demand upon ourselves which is *a priori* and overriding, namely the demand that we shall become fully individuated, free, responsive and purely-spiritual subjects. God is that, and when we have become what is demanded of us we are united with God. Then we are spirit as God is spirit.

What does it mean to say that God is spirit? Originally spirit was a power or activity. It was thought of somewhat as a totally unscientific person might think of wind or electricity. It was an invisible pervasive sacred force that might enter people and cause them to act, for good or ill, in ways outside their ordinary range of behaviour. So spirit was thought of as supernatural because people under its influence surpass themselves, and in connection with its presence words like inspiration, grace, possession and charisma were used. The metaphors are physical: spirit enters people rather as air enters their lungs or water goes down their throats, and those who are filled with spirit are much more than usually roused, active, excitable, energetic, talented and commanding.

Two things follow from this. The first is that it is not quite correct to speak of spirit merely as a capacity, for one ought to add that it is an *extraordinary* capacity of persons. Because it is extraordinary it is portrayed mythologically as a force or energy that is poured into a person from outside him. It is not 'literally' that, for spirit is not any empirically-detectable physical energy. I have briefly defined it elsewhere as 'the power of transcendence'. More fully, spirit is the capacity to exceed one's natural capacities, the power of self-knowledge and self-transcendence. Spirit is that we can wholly surpass ourselves, which is why Kierkegaard can call spirit a relation, a way in which the self relates itself to itself. What this means is perhaps best shown by contrasting it with the way an animal lives, for an animal lives immersed in its own nature and acts out its own nature; it simply is itself and is not at any remove from itself. It is soulish and it does have intra-natural freedom to explore, to learn and so on; but it does not have freedom from nature and so it does not transcend nature through self-transcendence, for it just is identical with itself. It has intra-natural freedom to act within the limits of its own natural capacities, but it does not have supernatural freedom, the capacity to exceed its natural capacities, for only a person, a being that can become spirit, has that.

Secondly, if spirit is a supernatural capacity (namely the capacity entirely to exceed one's natural capacities, the power of self-transcendence) are there any beings who are purely spirits – just spiritual, so that their being spirit is their essence?

It is very difficult to see how this can be so. The difficulty is rather like that which one feels over Aristotle's God, who was supposed to be purely self-absorbed self-thinking thought. There is nothing for such a being to think, nothing indeed for such a being to be, for how can a being be nothing but its own – inevitably contentless – thought of itself? The idea is surely as empty as St Thomas' doctrine that God is his own existence because what God is is merely that God is. Similarly, how can an individual being be nothing but its own relation of transcendence to itself? There is nothing for it to transcend. Surely only a being that is already something else, that already has a nature, can have superadded to it the power of self-transcendence? So the idea of an individual pure spirit appears to be an empty idea. There cannot be a free-floating pure spirit. There can only be something's becoming spirit. So spirit exists only in persons who have become spirit. In them it is self-transcendence, but it is not a transcendent being apart from them.

Yet most of mankind in the past have certainly supposed that there were such things as individual spirit-beings. How could they think such a thing if, as I have suggested, the idea of an individual spirit-being is empty? It seems that when they experienced spiritual powers within themselves they naturally supposed themselves to have been entered by spirit-beings. They personified the new capacities they had acquired. We still have a great many idioms describing states in which one seems to oneself to have an intruding alien personality within oneself. For example:

I don't know what's come over me.

The devil's in me tonight!

I don't know what made me do it.

He fought like a man possessed.

And it is still exceedingly common for people to speak of inspiration, influence, the Muse, grace, possession and so forth. C. G. Jung has described in detail how readily elements in the psyche can take on the aspect of distinct personalities. The literary form of allegory reflects this fact, for allegory personifies forces, virtues and motives that are in dialogue or conflict with each other within the self; though it is noticeable that we today are much less inclined than were our ancestors to think in such ways.

The reason why most of mankind in the past have believed in individual spirits seems then to be that if I am in an unusual mood or feel I am in possession of unusual powers I very readily personify as an intruder or visitant from outside this unusual element within myself. The human mind simply works like that, so much so that many preliterate cultures believed in a plurality of souls in everybody. Today, since the Enlightenment, we are generally less inclined to think in animistic ways, and in particular we are much less inclined to perceive strange elements within ourselves as intrusive spirits, foreign or visitant personal beings possessing us.

With this very important cultural change has come an increased awareness of an ancient difficulty: how can one tell spirits apart? Suppose we grant that there are spirits, that spirits are known by what they do, and that we are justified in blaming evil spirits for unpleasant happenings. Still, so far as anyone can tell, all evil spirits presumably get up to much the same sorts of unpleasant tricks, and nobody I think claims that you can learn to distinguish the handiwork of individual evil spirits. So how could we ever hope to be able to tell one spirit from another? Is there, for example, one big Devil or can we discriminate many little demons? One old answer was to the effect that spirits have names, and you can identify an individual spirit by pronouncing the correct name, that is, the one that you find gives you power over that individual demon, or wins you the favour of that individual deity. But I think no one will seriously propose that solution now, and the general problem of identifying spirits applies to all classes of disembodied persons or quasi-personal beings whether they be angels, demons, the souls of the dead or gods. To complete this argument, if we cannot see how we could ever reliably tell them apart, how can we be justified in claiming that there actually are distinct individual spirit-beings? We are making a claim that we can never substantiate nor put to practical use.

We have been discussing the meaning of spirit and what it might mean to say that God is spirit, and we have reached the apparently paradoxical and disappointing conclusion that spirit is only a capacity of persons (a capacity to exceed one's capacities, a capacity of complete self-knowledge and self-transcendence) and that – at least, so far as we are concerned – it does not seem to make sense to suppose that there can exist a being that is pure spirit and nothing else. For how can there be a pure subsistent relation of transcending without any 'matter' or nature that is transcended? It seems not to make sense to say that the transcending *is* the nature. So it appears that we are forced back to the point from which we began, namely that for us there is no god but the religious requirement: the imperative *Become spirit*! is the presence of God within us, and for us it is God, it is the goal as well as the requirement. For the requirement, as it bears upon us, awakens divine spirituality within us and so brings about the indwelling of the divine spirit – not as a distinct substance but as a metaphorical way of speaking about those supernatural capacities.

This is not as strange as it may seem, for it is after all the teaching of the prophets. They held that to know the divine requirement and to have internalized it *is* to know God. For us human beings there is no knowledge of God but the knowledge of the requirement, and for the prophets it was a blessed, longed-for state of affairs that one should have the divine requirement written within one's heart as an immanent or internalized commandment. Thus to have the divine law written within one's heart, they declared, would be to have the divine spirit poured out within oneself, it would be to have God living within one's heart. For them the radical internalization of religious realities and of the religious demand which I have been describing – and which the reader has doubtless been thinking to be some sort of reductionism, some sort of diminished version of religious realities – for them all this was the goal of religious development, because only along these lines can heteronomy or alienation between God and man be overcome. The objectified law written on tablets of stone had proved a failure and must be replaced by a new mode of knowledge of the divine will in which the way the divine requirement constrains us becomes so fully internalized that it becomes a demand that we make upon ourselves. My will and God's will coincide.

Now we run into the familiar paradox which has become such a feature of the religious debate in modern times, and I shall state it in the baldest form:

Preacher: You must internalize!

Philosopher: Internalization is atheism!

In a word, religion moves by its own inner momentum towards a condition which the philosophers consider to be atheism. In this way it seems to some shrewd outsiders that religion's inner logic is suicidal.

For at the heart of any great religious tradition will be found the insistence that the self can only attain its fullest emancipation and spiritual liberation by radically internalizing religious objects and themes. To use Christian language, it will be said that, merely as objective historical data, Christ's birth and death have no saving power and are of no religious interest. They become divine and saving only in their subjective appropriation, as Christ is born in me, dies in me, rises in me. Subjectivity is the only true divinity, for only as I take religious realities to heart and make them wholly my own do I discover what religious truth is. And the specifically religious requirement is just this demand, that I shall achieve spiritual liberation by wholly internalizing religious objects such as God, Christ, the spirit and so on. It is only by internalizing religious ideals that I can attain them.

Although this theme has been expressed with the most outstanding force by Luther, Kierkegaard and some of their modern followers, it has always been present in the tradition. It is implicit in the Jewish prophets' hope, explicit in Paul's Christ-mysticism, and a constant topic of devotional writers. If theology takes it seriously, then theology must shift from an objective to a subjective and internalized interpretation of Christian doctrines. Then it is that complaints of reductionism and atheism begin to be made.

There is no way of avoiding this vulnerable position. It is too deeply rooted in scripture and the tradition. For the law, the prophets and the psalmist tells us not to worship idols and not to rely upon any objective expression or sign of God's reality and fidelity. One of the worst heresies was considered to be the belief that there can be theoretical knowledge of God. In opposition to it the mainstream of tradition said that faith in God is a cleaving to the impenetrable divine mystery in non-cognitive practical obedience. The only way to know God was to decide for God and to obey God.

So in our argument we have run pretty close to the old doctrine. 'So far as you are concerned', the prophets said, 'there is no knowledge of God but the doing of the will of God.' They had faintly absurd ideas of how to ascertain God's will – you inquired of Yahweh by means of an ephod, or Urim and Thummim, or an entranced holy man – and I have replaced the expression 'the will of God' by 'the religious requirement'. But the teaching comes out much the same. There is so far as we are concerned no God but the religious requirement, the choice of it, the acceptance of its demand and the liberating self-transcendence it brings about in us.

Is that atheism? How does it differ from the old doctrine? I think it will be said that there is a crucial difference over the question of the personality of God, the grace of God, the divine initiative and the divine love. For often in the old 'literal' personal theism God's will was disclosed, God's judgment fell and God's blessing was bestowed *ad hoc*. You could almost say God improvised, made up his own mind on the spur of the moment and was subject to fits of moodiness, savagery and tender mercy. Such a God was not dull to live with. He was exuberantly and outrageously 'personal'. By contrast, the religious requirement is an impersonal categorically-binding unconditional principle against which we bounce ourselves, and which breaks and remakes us simply by being itself so utterly unyielding. It is the immutability of God, his eternal silent waiting without batting an eyelid, that forces us to confess everything. What an interrogator! He does not lift a finger and yet he gets everything he wants.

Yes, there *is* considerable change here, and it is of course the changeover from a descriptive to an expressive use of religious language. I am religious, I have freely chosen to live under the religious requirement, and it is in fact highly dramatic so to live, but the drama has become internalized. In the Old Testament it was God who appeared to be posturing dramatically, and the believer hid in the cleft of the rock, kept his head down, remained very still and hoped that the divine storm would soon blow itself out. Today God keeps still – and I jump. For as we have seen in the course of the discussion, when I bind the religious requirement unconditionally upon myself it so affects me that I quite properly and meaningfully describe it as waiting, as searching me out, as judging and condemning me, as restoring me, freeing me, and as filling me with divine spirit. So the relation to the religious requirement is personal, in that it generates a highly dramatic religious life in the believer. But I do not anthropomorphically project the personal characteristics into the requirement itself, for to do so would be to fall into the pathetic fallacy. So far as we can tell, there is no objective personal God. The old language is still used, but the modern believer should use it expressively rather than descriptively. Again, the modern form of faith has deep roots in the tradition. For it was always said first that God is immutable and impassible and secondly that he cannot be spoken of or known directly but only in terms of his effects. We have taken full account of both these points. So again, if you judge my view atheistic please acknowledge also that it has an approximately equal claim to be judged orthodox and I shall be satisfied. Meanwhile I maintain that we have no way of judging that there is a god who is a person,

who takes the initiative and so forth, for the personal language
that we use is expressive of the effect of the religious requirement
upon us, and it is mere sentimentality to project it upon that silent,
unconditional, unchanging demand. For it seems that the religious
requirement in itself is not a personal being but a categorical
imperative principle.

Many people claim that God acts. But talk of God's action
belongs only within the context of religious language and imagery.
Nowadays not even the most conservative believers can claim to
be able to deploy the idea of divine action effectively in the fields
of natural and social science, politics and economics. Tacitly, the
point has been conceded that talk of divine action belongs to the
expressive language of religion. For what is the evidence that God
acts? People refer to the witness of sacred writings, and to a 'feeling
of givenness', that is, the fact that in the drama of the religious life
it feels as if we are acted upon by, and as if we find ourselves
responding to, the action of Another. That is undoubtedly true, for
monotheists at least, but we have seen how this 'feeling' is generated. The religious requirement is itself unconditional, categorical
and immutable. It acts only in the pickwickian sense that it produces a whole spectrum of remarkable effects in us just by being
itself so unbending. Struggling with its silent unyielding demand
– 'You must change your whole life. That is the only way to
spiritual integrity and freedom from this false and ugly self that
you are, for at present your very selfhood is a pack of lies!' –
confronted with such a demand and accepting it, we find that it is
utterly searching, condemning, reviving, forgiving and gracious.
We may well find ourselves using the rich expressive vocabulary of
religion in order to tell what is happening to us. We speak of the
judgment and mercy of God, and we are right to do so – provided
we accept the expressive character of the language. It does not
show nothing, as is sometimes mistakenly supposed; but what it
shows is not what God is like, but what the human response to
God is like. It expresses the structure of the human religious life.
God acts only in the sense that he produces effects in us – by being
immutable.

We can now summarize the view of God we have arrived at –
a view which aims to be non-metaphysical and adequate to religious reality.

God is the central, unifying symbol of the religious life. The
unconditional religious requirement ('the will of God') is an autonomous inner imperative that urges us to fulfil our highest possible

destiny as spiritual, self-conscious beings emerging from nature. The requirement is *not* purely immanent, because it is not merely a demand that we fulfil the immanent teleology of our own present natures; on the contrary, it requires self-transcendence and victory over nature. Hence the appropriateness of the symbol of a transcendent being who imposes it; and he not only imposes it but also represents the goal towards which it directs us, for God is pictured as being already sovereign over nature ('the creator of the world'), with the highest degree of spirituality and self-awareness ('life, spirit'), freedom and love.

Thus God is both the beginning and the end of the religious life, and the various things that are said of and to God by believers are all rooted in various phases or moments of the inner life. This traditional expression, 'the inner life', is in truth rather misleading; what is meant is that when the religious requirement imposes upon us its own unconditional authority it plunges us into a kind of mythic drama of considerable violence. That mythic drama is the so-called inner life, and religious language is founded in it. For example, the religious requirement demands an entire change in our whole way of life. Nothing is allowed to escape it. It searches out everything. From this experience is derived talk about the eye of God, and about the omniscience of God.

But much of what the requirement searches out and brings to light is just the material that we would have preferred to keep hidden (God sifts, weighs in the balance and judges). And the call to become spirit, the call to intensified individuality, self-awareness and self-transcendence on the way to perfect emancipation from natural necessity and perfectly disinterested spirituality – this call requires a death and a loss of the old false self. God is experienced as judging and condemning us before he is experienced as bringing us to new life. So the religious demand pushes believers through the ancient psychodrama of the descent into the underworld, the passage through darkness to light, through death to life. Our typical language about God is simply the script for this drama, as the Hebrew psalter makes so clear.

Thus for a monotheist God is that about which the religious life revolves and – to put it another way – the phrase 'the relation to God' encompasses all the vast and turbulent emotional range of the religious life. The religious requirement itself is simply a principle, very like a Kantian categorically-imperative principle, which we are able to recognize in virtue of our capacity for self-transcendence and liberation from natural necessity. It commands us to seek the full completion of something which ordinarily is ours only in a very small and partial way; a completion which in the language of religion is given such names as salvation, eternal life, beatitude and so forth. We use the word 'God' as a comprehensive symbol that incorporates the way the religious demand presents itself to us (God's will), its ideal fulfilment by us (God's essence), and the mythic psychodrama that envelops us on the way (God's action).

Inevitably the question will be put, 'Does God exist outside faith's relation to God, or is the concept of God just a convenient heuristic fiction that regulates the religious life?' The crucial point about this often-asked question[3] is that it is of no religious interest. There cannot be any religious interest in any supposed extra-religious reality of God, and I have argued all along that the religious requirement's authority is autonomous and does not depend upon any external imponent. The authority of the religious requirement has to be autonomous and intrinsic in order that it may be fully internalized, imposed by us freely upon ourselves and made our own.

Why? – Because it is a contradiction to suppose that my highest spiritual freedom could be determined for me from without, and by the act of another. It must be actualized within me through the operation of an autonomous and intrinsically-authoritative principle that commands me to seek it, a principle that I make my own, that I confess as Lord and make the governing principle of my own life. If my salvation is my highest spiritual liberation then the God who gives it and the 'I' who receive it must coincide in the act of realizing it.

So it would seem that religion forbids that there should be any extra-religious reality of God. The most we can say is that it is religiously appropriate to think that there may be beyond the God of religion a transcendent divine mystery witnessed to in various ways by the faith of mankind. But we cannot say anything about it. Any possibility of a non-religious knowledge of this mystery would weaken the stringency and the saving power of the religious requirement. The religious requirement is for the transformation of the self and not for theoretical or speculative illumination. So no more than the merest chink of openness to the possibility of objective theism is permissible. The traditional emphasis on the negative way, on *agnōsia* or unknowing, was at its best an attempt to inhibit the development of a metaphysical theology and to safeguard the primacy of religion. Today we do not have a well-established metaphysical theology and cannot create one, so we should be glad to be spared the temptation to do so. In practice we have to make do with the use of the word 'God' as an incorporating or unifying symbol connoting the whole of what we are up against in the spiritual life.

8

HOW REAL SHOULD GOD BE?

We have reversed the traditional order. In the old belief, first you asserted that God existed and had such-and-such attributes, and then you claimed that since there is such a God it is fitting to worship him and to commit your whole life to him.

The difficulty with that traditional scheme is that we do not now have sufficient evidence that an objective God exists. Indeed the whole question is shrouded in such a degree of doubt and uncertainty that it is impossible to see how we could ever resolve it with enough confidence to be justified in committing our whole lives upon the outcome. The evil in the world is very great and we see little or no reliable evidence of a benevolent providence, and besides, the principle of autonomy suggests that such a commitment would in any case be morally dubious. Strangely enough, the more literally I imagine a supracosmic being to exist the less he seems to have to do with religion.[1]

So we have reversed the order, putting spirituality first and God second, somewhat as the Buddha put the Dharma above the gods. That is, on our account the religious imperative that commands us to become free spirit is perceived as an autonomously authoritative principle which has to be freely and autonomously adopted and self-imposed. We choose to be religious because it is better so to be. We must strive with all our might to become spirit, and what God is appears in the striving to answer this call. God is, quite simply, what the religious requirement comes to mean to us as we respond to it.

A religion is a cluster of spiritual values. Though the requirement is universal, the way in which it is experienced and the value-cluster are somewhat different in different traditions; not so widely different as religions are at the level of doctrine, but nonetheless significantly different. There are even religions whose value-cluster is such that for them theistic faith is not the appropriate expression of what it is to live subject to the requirement. However, in the forms of faith presently under discussion it does appear that the unifying symbol 'God' is a very powerful and apt expression of what it is that the believer finds himself up against in the religious life. We shall soon analyse in more detail what this qualified form of theism involves.

At any rate on our account the religious requirement comes first and God comes second. If it be objected that this is not what a man like Aquinas believed, I answer that naturally it is not what Aquinas believed for if Aquinas were alive today not even he himself could contrive to believe what his thirteenth-century self believed. In those days it was reasonable to believe that the sun circled the earth, but it is not reasonable so to believe today; and in those days of Aristotelean physics it was reasonable to believe in objective theism, but it is not reasonable so to believe today for there is not sufficient evidence. Times have changed, and one can only express what faith is today with the means available today. Modern believers cannot be expected to believe in the style of the sixteenth or thirteenth centuries.

Earlier generations of doubters – for example, many Victorians – roughly divided Christianity into two parts, the doctrine and the ethics. The doctrine, they said, is regrettably not true but we can and will retain the morality. But there is something else more important than either the doctrine or the ethics, and that is the spirituality. It is the spirituality that must not be lost. In the past it underlay and determined both the doctrine and the ethics. They (the doctrine and the ethics, that is) will come out very differently today, inevitably, but at least if the underlying spirituality can be saved the essential continuity of the tradition will have been maintained. Realism supposes that the chief criteria of identity and continuity are to be found in the area of doctrine. But they are not, for spirituality is more fundamental. It is the least obtrusive and hardest to grasp of the various dimensions of religion, but it is the key to all else.

Mention of the possibility of non-theistic religion reminds us that we have to make out a new kind of case for theism. Is theism religiously a good thing at all, and just how real will strictly religious considerations permit God to be?

This is a strange question. Perhaps the first person to raise it (at

least by implication) was Kant, and it is still novel and unsettling.
I mean this: in an important sense God is for the sake of religion
and not the other way round, so that just how real it is right for
God to be is for religious criteria to determine. A very approximate
sketch of a solution will illustrate some of the relevant considerations: to personify God gives the human subject a personal an-
tagonist to struggle against and helps to accelerate the growth of
the human person, his spirituality and self-awareness. More elements of the personality are drawn into the spiritual life, which
thus becomes more dramatic. It is good to have a personal God to
fight for the same sort of reason as it is better to be married than
single, so that at this point monotheism has a considerable advantage over Buddhism. On the other hand, a personal God easily
comes too far forward into objectivity and turns into a benevolent
despot whose influence is regressive. He becomes confused with
kindly, protective and inhibiting parent-figures, tempts the believer
back into the security of infancy, and blocks the development of
autonomous mature spirituality. Backsliding into anthropomorphism and superstition easily occurs. So some kind of balance needs
to be struck between the advantageous and the disadvantageous
features of belief in a personal God. In particular, as we progress
in the religious life God must steadily withdraw. Spiritual matur-
ation requires a gradual relinquishing of the consolations of
religion as God becomes less a person, more a principle.

However, we must spell out in a little more detail how life
subject to the religious requirement generates belief in God.

The religious requirement itself is 'the will of God', for God was
always known first and foremost as an imperative, a command.
The formal features of the requirement are the basis of talk about
God's 'quiescent' or metaphysical attributes. For example, the requirement is absolute and unchanging (God's immutability), autonomously and intrinsically authoritative (God's aseity), and even
infinite, for it is experienced precisely as a call to break out of the
finite – the rut, the groove, the little cycles of habits into which we
long to settle, fold our hands and slumber. We hate boundlessness
and would much prefer to stay within the comfortable limits of
our present natures, regardless of the fact that we understand
perfectly well that to do so is to find those limits steadily contract-
ing. To stay within the limits of our own nature is death. Habit
kills, for it slowly puts one to sleep spiritually. The requirement
says that for a human being, unlike an animal, there is no life
except by a ceaseless struggle after self-transcendence and becom-

only certain aspects

ing spirit. This is undoubtedly very taxing, but all developed religious traditions place a high value on wakefulness, vigilance and alertness. They have commonly expressed puritanical disapproval of alcohol, sexual excitement, music and strong emotion, because of their drugging effects. Spirituality demands a sustained high *disagree* level of recollected and supple self-awareness. Hence God is described as self-thinking thought that never slumbers nor sleeps: God's maximal spiritual alertness and vitality is a representation of the ideal to be aimed at.

God's simplicity and eternity represent to us other features of the religious requirement. Somehow everyone seems to know without being told that the more your soul is scattered or dispersed over external objects, worries and desires, the further you are from religion. You are not capable of religious reflection – a kind of quiet watchfulness – when you are inwardly so confused and dissipated. Religion is inner clarity and simplicity. Nothing is further from religion than the flustered 'involvement' and busyness which in some quarters passes for Christian ethics. In fact, most people recognize (again without being told) that compulsive altruism, so far from being an authentic religious expression, is a symptom of a flight from religion. Those who are inwardly lost and alienated from themselves conceal their own inner despair by living for others, and the irony of their situation makes them the subject of many jokes. 'She lives for others, and you can tell the others by their hunted looks.' 'We were put on this earth to help others' – 'And what were the others put on this earth for?'

So both Christianity and Buddhism traditionally and correctly insisted that one's first concern must be for one's own salvation. And since God is the personification of what spirituality requires to us, God himself was accordingly said to be simply self-possessed and eternally and necessarily to will and to love himself. The crucial point is that in the traditional picture God's infinite love, creativity and self-outpouring are based on his aseity and his willing himself and loving himself. You cannot give it unless first you have it. God's simplicity, or lucid self-possession, is the foundation of God's absolute power of self-giving. Again we see that *the doctrine of God is an encoded set of spiritual directives*.

God's eternity is also best approached indirectly or negatively. We are often further from religion when we are most trapped in time and absorbed in the ephemeral (literally, that which endures only for a day). Mere temporality draws us away from religion in several different ways. For example, many people waste most of

the best years of their lives toiling away in the attempt to make
their last years financially secure, and others are involved in oc-
cupations (such as the fashion, marketing and communications
businesses) which chain them to the study of the fleeting whims of
Demos – an intriguing topic, but spiritually dissipating: 'Vanity',
it used to be called. Others again find that Eros is haunted by fear
of the passage of time and the relentless approach of betrayal,
corruption, loss and death. By contrast, the religious requirement
is quite indifferent to time. Neither the past nor the future concern
it. The eternal is the present moment, as if the clock had stopped
or as if the first stroke of midnight were just sounding. And the
requirement never varies by one iota for it cannot possibly become
either any more or any less imperative than it is. It is not in its
nature to vary. Thus it was always said and is obviously true that
one should pray without ceasing and attend unchangingly to the
unchangeable God, and every religious person knows that the
requirement is just as much present while one is fast asleep as while
one is awake. I testify that I am aware of it while I am asleep. As
a matter of fact if one is a religious person one cannot help but
pray without ceasing; there is no choice. So we instantly recognize
what is meant by religious writers such as Augustine, Calvin and
Newman when they say that it is for them as if nothing exists
except God and the soul.

From all this it is easy to see how talk of God's quiescent or
metaphysical attributes is simply an expression of what it is to be
religious. For one who acknowledges the requirement, it is as if he
is up against something which has these attributes. Theism is a
mythical (and valuable) representation of how the requirement
appears to someone subject to it.

However, the requirement is a principle and not a substance and
I do not intend in the course of the argument surreptitiously to
convert it into a substance. So it may be said, 'What about talk of
God's operative attributes and God's actions? Does not the main
line of argument eliminate the reality of God's action, initiative
and Grace?'

However, we are no worse off here than the objective theists.
For traditional theism makes three claims, as follows:

(*i*) God is active;

(*ii*) God is immutable; and

(*iii*) God is in this life known only through his effects.

How can these three claims be reconciled? It would seem that if an
account of God must be such that these three things can all be said

of him, then something like our own account has to be given. For on our account God is not really a person or a substance but (so far as we are concerned) an unconditionally demanding and inflexible principle which as we choose it and lay it upon ourselves generates certain effects within us; theistic faith, the drama of the spiritual life and so on. Thus we resolve the antinomy by saying that God is omnipotently wise, searching, gracious and active – in his very immutability. God is wise and all-knowing, in the way in which the religious requirement is experienced by us as searching our hearts, because its demand for spiritual integrity will not allow us to keep any drawers locked. Everything must be exposed and brought to light. Again, God is holy in that the religious requirement is exalted above and is unaffected by any mundane considerations whatever. Its demand for inner purity and integrity is unconditional. Hence, for example, Jesus' quite 'unreasonable' condemnation of lustful and angry thoughts. God is true in the sense that the requirement lays bare or exposes the truth with complete authority, and in the sense that the moral truth or integrity it requires of us and insists upon creating in us is of supreme and rocklike worth. God is powerful in the sense that the religious requirement recreates us from nothing (it reduces us to dust and then remakes us of dust), and God is just in that the religious requirement is not – and could not conceivably be – any respecter of persons. God is Spirit, pure self-awareness, unsleeping self-thinking thought in that the religious requirement has the power to make us Spirit, so that we naturally credit God with archetypal possession of the sovereign spiritual lightness, freedom and mastery which we gain through the relation to him. Finally, God is creator in this sense, that the call to become Spirit makes me aware of the limits within which I formerly lived. At that moment I realize that I have been stuck in nature, in bondage to limit. I had sentenced myself to finitude and was on the way to death. To become spirit I have to die to death by breaking out of that old habit-bound, decaying and egotistical self and letting myself be created anew. Because I have to cease being a painfully self-limited self and to let myself become spirit, the basic disposition I need in order to achieve salvation is simple receptivity and self-surrender. When I become nothing, then I experience salvation as pure gift, creation out of nothing, and the fact that it is so experienced is doubtless the most important single motive for a theistic interpretation of the spiritual life.

However, the religious requirement is a principle and not a

substance. Maybe there are features of the religious life that naturally suggest that in encountering it we deal with a personal God.
But there are other features which point the other way. The God
of religious faith may be thought of as a person but if so then the
qualification has to be added, 'But God is an unchangeable person,
an eternal person who cannot be bent, who yields to no persua-
sions.' An unchangeable person is scarcely in the usual sense a
person at all. For consider the story that follows.

A traveller arrives one day at a village on the edge of hill-country.
He had intended to continue on his journey, but finds that beyond
the village his way is blocked by an immense and utterly impassable
mountain. Nothing daunted, he settles in the village to wait. Years
pass and his head whitens. Finally he dies, but he is long remem-
bered in the village as a proverb: 'The man who waited for the
mountain to move.' Generations, and then centuries, come and go.
Finally the population moves away and the village is uninhabited.
Slowly the buildings crumble and topple; the stones fall to the
ground, sink and are split by frost and roots. Eventually all trace
of the village is obliterated – and still the mountain has not changed
one iota. That is what it is like to have to do with an unchangeable
God.[2]

Again, suppose we take a political analogy, and compare the
relative merits of living under personal rule and living under the
rule of law. Surely the rule of law is infinitely to be preferred,
however wise and good and enlightened the despot may be? However good the despot, life under personal rule is inevitably bad for
everybody's morals. Under personal rule, for example, bribery is
morally normal because the hierarchical order must be ritually
confirmed by the movement of gifts and patronage up and down
the line – and a good deal of worship, if understood literally, is
busy doing precisely that. But no one who has lived under the rule
of universal and impartial law would wish to return to life under
personal rule. Now if God is wise and good, God will not need
telling that life under his personal rule would be morally corrupting
if he were ever to be in any respect arbitrary, capricious, flexible
or discriminatory. If God ever gives way to special pleading, the
rot sets in. We will all start wheedling and we will all want to be
treated as special cases. So the most morally-effective personal rule
will necessarily be the rule which is entirely lawlike and never
respects persons. And is not God in fact said to be absolutely just
and no respecter of persons? This in effect means that God is not
partial or personal, but presents himself to us in the religious life

as one who is a principle and not a person. For a life governed by principles is spiritually freer and more advanced than a life under personal rule, just as there is such a thing as 'freedom under the law' but there is no such thing as freedom under even the very best of absolute monarchs. So if God is really good and wills what is best for us, then God as cosmic superperson or Heavenly Father must bow out and give place to God as law-like inflexible requirement that we become free and fully-mature autonomous spiritual individuals. If we are to achieve that destiny then, in the modern phrase, God must keep a very low profile.

This point of view resolves an ancient and (as I think) very severe difficulty in the idea of God. For in popular traditional belief God acts at two levels, or in two different ways, which do not consort well together. It is suggested that on the large scale God functions in a regular or lawlike manner, while in addition occasionally revealing also that he is personal by the way he intervenes *ad hoc* on the small scale. The two different ideas of God – the regular cosmic God and the small-scale, interventionist, personal God – do not fit well together and never did. But theologians have felt that they must keep both and must try to synthesize them because God was after all supposed to be both universal and also in some sense personal.

Perhaps the difficulty arose historically through the inflation of a small tribal deity into the cosmic creator of Graeco-Roman culture. Today's small personal God, who fixes answers to prayer, miracles, portents and little banes and blessings in response to the needs of individual believers, is a relic of the god of a small-scale pre-philosophical society. He has lingered on into modern times not merely because he is so comforting to the superstitious, but also because he is thought to be necessary in order to stop the large-scale cosmic deity from evaporating into bland vagueness.

For the action of the large-scale cosmic deity is universal, equal and invariable. God is thought of as omnipresent in his roles of creator, sustainer and providential orderer. Omnipotent and omniscient, he is present and active in just the same way and to just the same degree at every point in the whole universe. But then, if God's general action and presence are so equal and invariable is he not in danger of becoming indiscernible, like the music of the spheres in medieval times? How can you pick out or discriminate a power that is unalterably and everywhere necessarily just the same? If God is everything in general like that, perhaps we had better forget him and concentrate our own efforts on becoming something in particular. For a divine presence and action which is so perfectly equable in all the ups and downs of life is no longer worth troubling with. God never really makes his presence felt.

These questions presented themselves very forcibly in the age of the Enlightenment. Several of the leading philosophers, including Spinoza and Leibniz, had rejected ideas of special divine intervention as superstitious and incompatible with the greater and more important belief in the divine governance of all events by cosmic law; and the Deists in particular accepted this argument. But the Deists' God turned out to be unable to survive on his own. Those occasional interventions had been vital to sustain the belief that God was a distinct individual personal being; without them God simply faded out into pantheism, naturalism and atheism. The minimal God of Voltaire and Hume vanished altogether a generation or so later.

The same story was re-enacted in the controversy between catastrophists and uniformitarians in geology in the early nineteenth century. The catastrophists were holding out for a personal interventionist God. The uniformitarians both won the scientific argument and claimed, in many cases, to stand for a larger conception of God.[3] But the God of uniformitarianism quickly faded from the earth sciences and the life sciences. They did not need that hypothesis.

So here is the paradox: we need the little interventionist God to give personal qualities to the universal God and to stop him from fading into emptiness and vacuity. Conversely, the lawlike cosmic God is needed to give breadth and universality to the little interventionist God and stop *him* from declining into a fantasy guardian-spirit. But the two deities, the big one and the little one, are quite different from each other. They presuppose different cultural backgrounds, different overall views of the cosmic order and how it is maintained, and different views of God's relation to man. Neither view of God will do on its own. They need each other – and yet they do not go well together.

Side by side then (and both of them taken a good deal too literally) God's lawlike aspect and his personal aspect do not fit at all well together. Our account unifies them: God's lawlike aspect is a principle, the religious requirement, and God's personal aspect is a mythical representation (valuable in many ways) of the requirement's effect and impact upon us. God's lawlike and personal aspects respectively represent to us the demand and the promise of the spiritual life. While God's lawlike aspect remained bound to the perceived cosmic order it was in danger of losing religious effectiveness. Such a God easily becomes a *deus otiosus* fading away into the blue yonder. But God's lawlike aspect comes into its own and gains its full religious power when it is internalized as an *a priori* principle.

We began with the question, How real should God be? We answer that objectively God must be quite indeterminable, for if God werc to bccomc in any way determinate he would restrict the freedom which is the essence of spirituality. Something of this point was recognized in the traditional insistence on the divine spirituality, infinity and incomprehensibility. Subjectively, God is indeed much more determinate, because in his subjective aspect he is a mythical representation of what the spiritual life requires of us and promises to us. As such he is an 'as if' whose spiritual value, great at first, thereafter diminishes.

9

IS THE RELIGIOUS IDEAL ATTAINABLE?

Gods personify religious values. A god is a spiritual being, energetic, lucid, creative and autonomous. A god has perfect self-knowledge and self-possession and so is not bound by nature but on the contrary controls nature. Thus all gods by definition meet the central religious requirement, that one should become free, sovereign and fully individuated spirit. A god simply is the imagined actuality of the religious ideal which we experience as summoning and commanding us. 'Be holy as I am holy', it says.

Here we have to make a distinction between the central and basic religious requirement that one should become spirit, and the total religious ideal. All gods meet the former, but in a polytheistic system the realization of the latter is done, not by any individual deity, but by the pantheon collectively. Each individual god specializes, concentrating on controlling some region of the cosmos or aspect of nature, and on exemplifying one or two of the subsidiary moral and religious virtues and values, such as justice or wisdom or skill in the arts or crafts.

There is merit in this arrangement. As a totemic system is said to be a mnemonic inventory of important features of the natural environment, so the pantheon of gods each with their special attributes presents believers with an ordered array of the desirable spiritual qualities and powers. Polytheism makes it plain that the central ideal that we should become spirit can be realized in many different ways, for one may direct one's devotions to this or that god or group of gods in accordance with one's own temperament and aptitudes. It is easy to select aspects of the total religious ideal for one's personal cultivation. David Hume was not being entirely facetious when he suggested that polytheism is preferable to monotheism, especially in large-scale societies, because it is more plural and tolerant and makes more allowance for human diversity.[1] The pantheon can be enlarged, and there may be changes in the relative power and popularity of its various members, all of which gives considerable flexibility.

However, in the pantheon there is no single individual in whom is realized the total religious ideal. It is distributed among many individuals who are not always in perfect harmony. So polytheism belongs to a stage in human development when consciousness is not yet fully unified, the cosmos is not yet fully unified, and the total religious ideal is not yet unified. These three things, the self, the world and God, always evolve in parallel with each as a kind of mirror of the others, and polytheism reflects a stage when cosmology and consciousness and are not yet fully clarified and unified. To put it in political terms, there are too many powerful barons out in the regions and the central government has not become strong enough yet to impose its own law upon the whole country.

But as thought develops, polytheism becomes inadequate. It fails to present a sufficiently unified cosmology and does not offer any inspiring image of the synthetic unification of the total religious ideal, realized within one infinite individual spirit. So when men begin to conceive of the cosmos as a single law-governed whole and of the self as a unity perspicuous to itself, the time has come for the transition to monotheism.

Now the old gods appear incomplete. They have shrunk in stature. Imagine that the entire pantheon has been enclosed or encapsulated within the infinite divine mind, so that the old gods have become no more than aspects or attributes of God. The ideal correlative of the human mind, that to which it relates itself and in which it perceives its own image and destiny, is now no longer one of the gods but the one God. And if the human mind's counterpart and ideal is now God, then the old gods are no more than mere elements in our psyches, allegorical figures. They still make themselves heard in our inner life, but they have lost their former final authority. They are voices which deserve a hearing, but they are not the one voice that has to be obeyed.

The transition from polytheism to monotheism clearly marks a huge advance in the human self's consciousness of itself and of its potentialities. The advance is precisely and exactly the advance from the pantheon to the God of monotheism, for a god is just a spiritual ideal that men aspire after and hope to attain. By their

gods ye shall know them: 'they that make them be like unto them'
(Ps. 135.18 RV).

Yet polytheism did have great fortitude in its realism about the
irrationality, disharmony and evil in life. It represented the tragic
contradictions of life as reflecting permanent conflicts between
different deities standing respectively for the principles of good and
evil, order and anarchy, justice and mercy and so on. At least in
this way life's conflicts were truthfully represented in the mythology, even if they were inevitably not resolved.

Sadly though, this failure to overcome evil and discord means
that polytheistic religion is often rather pessimistic – Egypt seems
to be the chief exception – about the destiny of the ordinary humble
individual. In the quarrelsome society of the gods, kings and great
heroes may be able to hold their own and be at ease, but the
common man prefers more peace and quiet. The Supreme Good is
not yet unified enough for him to feel that he can look forward to
a blessed immortality.

The element of tragic conflict in life, then, is the principal threat
to the common man's hope of salvation. It is worse than the threat
of physical suffering and worse than the threat posed by our own
moral wickedness, for it implies that the total religious ideal is
forever unattainable because it is incoherent. If there are among
the various moral and religious values that deserve our allegiance
some that are mutually irreconcilable, then it is impossible as they
say to 'get it all together'. There cannot be an actual being or state
of affairs which is the fullness of achieved perfection. There is no
final salvation and there cannot be just one God.

Polytheism seems to be saying this. Even the gods are not completely secure. They are subject to fate and although they do not
exactly die they may, like old soldiers, slowly fade away. Polytheism tells us that there are permanent and unresolved differences
within the divine realm, that is, basic conflicts of moral and religious ideals. If the divine realm is eternally divided there cannot be
one God. The connection between polytheism and pessimism in so
many cultures is not surprising, for suppose that by some miracle
I were to gain admission to the home of the gods; would I not be
devastated by the disputes between them?

Polytheism deserves our deep respect for the truthful and beautiful way in which the problem of evil is represented in its mythology; but simply because it is polytheism it cannot solve the
problem of evil. There just are many distinct gods, whose relations
with each other are not always cordial. By contrast, traditional

objective monotheism fails to give an adequate representation of the problem of evil and solves it by main force. The absolute unity of the divine realm in the simple and eternal perfection of God's nature is categorically asserted from the outset. We are told that it is logically impossible that there should be any internal conflict within the total religious ideal. Every perfection when raised to an infinite degree exactly coincides with every other, for in God all perfections are summed up and are identical in one simple and eternal substance. It may seem to us mortals that there is a *prima facie* tension between the claims of justice and mercy, and between the claims of love and personal liberty, but the appearance of conflict is merely superficial. Infinite justice, infinite mercy, divine love and divine freedom are all of them identical, and necessarily so, because there cannot be conflict in God.

Now from God's unity and perfection (i.e., his being the unified religious ideal) it follows according to orthodox theism that he is unchangeable and impassible. That is, he is without passions and so incapable of suffering. Not only that but, since sympathy or compassion is itself also a passion, God cannot experience *it* either. Compassion is fellow-feeling, and God is not our fellow and does not have feelings. To attribute the experience of suffering to God absolutely is the heresy of patripassianism.

In spite of this warning, many people recoil sharply from the passionless God of traditional belief and embrace patripassianism in the supposition that they are making only a minor modification in the received idea of God. Not so: for a dilemma can be demonstrated which proves that the suffering God is a different God.

The first horn of the dilemma is that an objectively existing and religiously-adequate God must by his very existence constitute a denial that there is in the end any such thing as the problem of evil. The second horn is that a God who *does* recognize and experience tragic conflict and spiritual affliction is not religiously-adequate and therefore is no God.

In the first horn of the dilemma mainstream orthodox theism faces the very severe challenge presented to it by moral tragedy. If our experience is riven with tragic contradictions, how can it be plausibly asserted that the world-ground is a simple synthesis of all perfections without any internal disharmony or conflict at all? There is nothing wrong with orthodox theism as an *ideal*. As we have seen in earlier chapters, it is an accurate mythical representation of the absolute religious requirement, its statements about God being nothing but disguised spiritual directives. Traditional theism is true – as an ideal; but if we insist upon saying that such a God actually exists we deny that moral evil and tragedy are anything more than superficial. Some forms of monotheism – Sunni Islam, perhaps? – seem to be quite uncompromising on this point, and brusquely override any objections as merely sentimental. Christianity is not so very different, for although it gives such prominence to its great tragic story of the passion of Christ, it traditionally insisted that this was only a human event. God does not suffer: he cannot.

In the second horn of the dilemma modern patripassian theism is found inadequate as a substitute for the older faith. During the past century a growing sense of the sheer vastness of human diversity, human evolution, and the long and still continuing tale of human suffering over the millenia has led to widespread revulsion against the traditional idea of God. It is now common for people to think of God as 'the great fellow-sufferer who understands' and who actually participates in the afflictions of his sentient creatures. Such ways of thinking took shape in the context of nineteenth-century humanitarian awareness of the historical struggle of the masses, and were sealed by the popular demand for adequate words of consolation in the face of the evils of the First World War. Thus in *The Hardest Part* (1918), G. A. Studdert-Kennedy writes: 'One needs a Father, and a Father must suffer in His children's suffering. I could not worship the passionless potentate . . . in their hearts all true men worship one God – the naked, wounded, bloody, but unconquered and unconquerable Christ. This is the God for whom the heart of democracy is longing, and after whom it is blindly, blunderingly, but earnestly groping.'[2]

Here then is a God who shares our troubles and experiences the same conflicts as we do. I suppose it is conceivable that there should be such a being, but is it not grotesque that God himself now fails to achieve the religious ideal? *God* is immersed in affliction, and struggles to achieve salvation! However comforting it may be to have so large a shoulder to cry on, such a being is as much in need of deliverance and victory over evil as we are. The god of the modern patripassian believer is nothing but Humanity, the god of Comtist humanism. Perhaps one may indeed obtain a kind of quasi-religious consolation from feeling one's own sufferings to be a small part of the still sad music of Humanity as a whole. There is a pre-echo of this humanist 'religion' in the beautiful line about Rachel weeping for her children and refusing to be comforted (Jer. 31.15). But it is not true religion, for it gains no permanent victory and no salvation.

So the suffering God of many modern believers may exist but is not religiously adequate. He is merely the tears and the fellow-feeling of humanity. There is no salvation in him. On the other hand the traditional metaphysical God is indeed religiously adequate, for he is simply the religious requirement itself in mythological form. But he is only an ideal. As such he is supremely powerful and authoritative and is often spoken of as 'existing' *a priori* or necessarily, rather as an *a priori* principle 'exists'. But this is to speak of existence in a stretched or analogically-extended way. God does not exist in a real or *a posteriori* sense.

The only religiously adequate God cannot exist. The world being what it is, he has to *be* ideal to function *as* the religious ideal. On the other hand the God in whom so many moderns instinctively believe, whom they suppose to be real and who in truth is merely a projection of human fellow-feeling, is not religiously adequate. That is the dilemma.

Oppressed by the large element of fantasy and the many unprovable claims in present-day religion, I have in this book chosen the way of the religious ideal. I make no metaphysical claims at all about God, life after death and so forth. Metaphysically, God's existence is *a priori*, like the existence of a principle. It is not 'real' existence. So it is fairest to say that on my account faith is a freely-undertaken commitment to live by certain values and subject to a particular standard.

The form of faith I myself adopt and recommend is Christian faith, but this choice need involve no unsubstantiated doctrinal claims. It will be quite sufficient to make a few checkable historical claims about the actual religious values that have been commended and pursued in the Christian tradition from the beginning. I have argued elsewhere that the key values, the most precious, can still as it happens be learnt direct from Jesus himself.[3]

Yet the problem of the unattainability of the religious ideal confronts my point of view quite as much as it does any other. If the tragic contradictions of existence are such that it is very hard to see how there can be an actual world-ground whose own nature unites all perfections without any internal conflict, is it not by the same token very hard to see how you or I can attain the religious ideal? Surely it does not happen in practice? Out in the real world every saint is deeply, deeply flawed. To name names, consider six outstanding modern figures: Kierkegaard, Dostoevsky, Tolstoy, Kafka, Simone Weil and Wittgenstein. They have several things in common, for they were neither priests nor theologians nor even conventionally-devout practising believers. They were heterodox figures on or beyond the outer fringes of institutional religion, but sharing a sort of sanctity, an attractive and fascinating intensity of moral and religious seriousness. At the same time all of them were disturbed personalities with, to put it mildly, substantial experience of psychic pain and distress. They could hurt those around them, but they suffered far worse themselves.

Such evidence as we have suggests that many of the great creative religious personalities of the past were similarly afflicted, at least in the Judaeo-Christian tradition.[4] (We do not know enough about the others.)

Does not all this suggest that the religious life is a matter of aspiration rather than attainment? What seems to mark an outstanding religious figure is the ardour of his religious longings rather than the serenity and security of his religious achievement. Untroubled, fully-achieved and victorious sanctity seems to be found only in the lying and propagandist pages of hagiography, not in the real world. In reality, the very religious mostly have a hard time.

You might object that the six persons above-named, like many others who could be quoted, were writers. Writers care only for the perfection of the work. Every writer will unhesitatingly choose to be an unhappy person who writes good books rather than a happy person who writes bad ones. A divided personality tormented by strong religious yearnings is very suitable for a writer and will help him to turn out good books, whereas quietly happy saints (if there are such unendurable beings) would certainly write rotten books. So the religious personalities we hear most of are the 'unhappy lovers' as Kierkegaard calls them. We hear so much of them not necessarily because they are in the majority but because they wail so loudly and eloquently that they insist on being heard.

So you might say, and you would have a point so far as the period of the Romantic Movement is concerned. But the tradition that the outstanding believer is a martyr or 'confessor' is well over two thousand years old. It is clear that Jeremiah and Ezekiel, Jesus and Paul had a very hard time without ever hearing about Romanticism.

Why? Why should major religious figures have a rougher ride than the rest of us? About the time of the Maccabean martyrs of the second century BC it came to be believed that their sufferings were such an affront that God was under a moral necessity to raise them from the dead and to reward them. But such giving of compensation does nothing to explain why the suffering was inflicted in the first place. And in any case the promise of a heavenly reward is only a mythological way of praising and recommending fidelity to religious ideals. Martyrdom has redemptive value in that the martyr bears precious witness to the supreme importance of religious values. That religious values mean so much to him encourages me to be faithful as well. So he inspires me to try to imitate his devotion.

Could a martyr really be faithful unto death to religious values, in the absence of any belief in post-mortem vindication? Well, those very first Maccabean martyrs must have been so faithful; and in any case are we not always telling each other that we really must learn to be disinterested? We have to learn to love things for their own sake and not for the sake of a personal reward. And of all the things that we must learn detachment from, the first is that frantic struggle to preserve and secure our own continuance.

So there is no life after death in the 'literal' sense, and here is a new or at any rate little-used argument to show it: *People are period pieces*. I am a twentieth-century English-speaking Westerner. I am what I am because of this context which has so largely made me what I am. If I lived in another century, another culture and another language-group, I would be a different person. My personal identity is a period piece. I am datable. Like an artefact I have a provenance, and so has every other human being who has ever lived. I would not be the same if I lived in another century, just as a work of art would not be the same if we were suddenly to discover that it belonged to a different century. His provenance is part of what constitutes a person's identity. He belongs to a certain milieu and cannot be abstracted from it.

That being so, it is clear that I cannot be the same person as, for example, a medieval Japanese. Even if I knew his language and culture very well, it would still be true that he has his provenance and I have mine. I could not identify him with myself, for his forms of thought and experience will not fit into the conceptual pigeonholes in my memory. I can learn him from the outside, but I cannot make him me, from the inside. The gulf is too great: what is his cannot be made mine.

We are aware of such gaps even between two different generations in the same language and culture, and between oneself speaking English and oneself speaking another language. But any life after death in another world must involve an immeasurably greater transition than the transition between me and the medieval Japanese. The Japanese and I have much in common, for we are members of the same biological species on the same planet, in the same time-order and both speaking natural languages. To make the transition to the next world we shall have to strip away all that and much more. Nothing at all will be left by which you could still recognize the old me, and my presumption must be that I would not be able to identify myself by my memories. For, to cite again the nearest possible analogy, I certainly could not remember the life of that Japanese as *my own* former life. *The way my memory works is also a period piece.* That is to say, what it will store, the way it stores it, and the way it refers to me what of mine it has stored, are all culturally conditioned, too. I can only remember as mine such things as can in principle become part of the experience of the twentieth-century English-speaking Westerner that I am. So the popular idea of reincarnation is nonsense, and I could not remember someone from an alien time and place as being none other than myself. How much more then is it impossible for me to suppose that one day another being, in another world altogether, will remember me as himself! I have no way of even beginning to imagine how such a thing could be.

The above argument may not rule out life after death altogether but it does at least show that we cannot confidently affirm it. For all practical purposes we must live as if there were no life after death, and seek to actualize religious values in this world as if there were no other. That means that if we choose to impose the religious requirement upon ourselves and to pursue religious values, it really must be for their own sakes that we do it. But is it rational to embrace religion, in view of the seemingly intense unhappiness of many of the most deeply religious and the consequent doubts about how far the religious ideal is attainable?

We can make a start here by distinguishing between the attainment of the religious ideal *tout court*, and its attainment by me. Usually, when we are thinking about these questions we think to ourselves, 'Look, if there is some great Good Time coming then I want my share in it or I shall turn nasty.' If we search our hearts we will discover, I fear, that that is what we think about life after death. But the religious ideal is that I shall become wholly disinterested. We can only find by losing, live by dying – we have heard the paradoxes so often that we have ceased to think about them. Yet they mean that I cannot attain the supreme good except by entirely renouncing the desire to attain it *for myself*. It is as if the

Supreme Good does not exist for me, but only in itself; which is perhaps another reason why God is represented as being 'self-existent', or 'from himself'. God cannot, as it were, be loved by me for my sake but only for his, for God is not for my sake but only for his. There is no God for me, or at least, not for this present me.

Why is this? It is curious how readily the phrase 'to love God' trips off people's tongues, for it is not a simple or easy idea. Do people have in mind a merely human affection for a treasured anthropomorphic image of God, a god who is a loved memento like a shabby teddy-bear that has survived from childhood? That is not the love of God. God offers me nothing that I can clutch to myself, and therefore cannot be loved with a subject-object love. I can only love God completely disinterestedly. If I can become purely disinterested, then that disinterestedness is sacred love and indeed is God: that is why God is love.

But in complete disinterestedness I no longer possess, own, or have for myself. The religious ideal, therefore, is not attainable *by me*, and it would perhaps be better not to speak of it as 'attainable' at all. It simply is, and is known only by entire and disinterested self-surrender into it. But this is extremely difficult and painful. The highest kind of religious happiness is outwardly entirely invisible. Only the affliction that it causes the natural ego is visible. The joy that is over the other side of loss is not visible, for it does not exist in any subject. It is a nirvana-joy.

Still, religious joy is a rare and very paradoxical thing and, since I am being so sceptical anyway, it could well be argued that for ordinary people like you and me the sceptic's sort of spirituality is easier and safer. At his best the sceptic is selfless, harmless and untroubled by death, and that is far more than most people achieve. I am none too bright and now that I am aproaching the teatime of life I will certainly not get any brighter. I am none too good and have observed that as they grow older most people get worse, so I am unlikely to become any better. Yet I have to face death. Would it not be more rational for me to settle for scepticism, which may be within my reach, rather than to aim for faith? Faith is after all so hard that Kierkegaard and Weil found it too hard even for them, so it is absurd for a lesser mortal even to think of attempting it. Why trouble with Christianity when it is such a difficult and indeed dubious way to happiness?

Scepticism is a safer way to peace of mind. The sceptic tells us to withold assent and remain uncommitted. That way we avoid error, distortion and the unhappiness of bigotry and fanaticism. Take pleasure in the flux of life, like a wise old Chinese poet and sage, and do not be so stupid as to make any demands upon yourself or others. To make such demands and to wish that things were other than they are is to court unhappiness and embitterment. Let be! Take pleasures easily and guiltlessly as they come and relinquish them without regret. Above all things avoid the company of true believers with their itch to change and improve, for they make life miserable.

Sceptics have a true spirituality and a kind of selflessness. At least, the sceptic says that a strongly principled and committed ego makes for unhappiness all round, and isn't he right? Not that the sceptic chooses a weak ego, a whining, dependent hysterical ego. Far from it. He has his own kind of fortitude. You have to work hard to acquire his complete absence of censoriousness and his lack of any hankering after the illusions of ideology. We should not hesitate to express sympathy for sceptical spirituality. <u>Too</u> <u>often the Western patriarchal monotheist has an ego like a clenched fist with whitened knuckles.</u> His affliction is not true religious affliction but merely a boring and trivial self-hatred which makes him spread misery all around him. The sceptic has an ego like water, which is in its own quiet way very durable. It is non-resistant and yielding. It is not fighting to hold itself together, like too many of the twice-born protestant egos one encounters nowadays.

What makes sceptical spirituality still more attractive is that the age of Christian dogmatism is clearly ending, and now perhaps the centuries of secular progress, ideology and the will to dominate nature are also coming to an end. Looking to Taoism, Buddhism and oriental landscape-painting one can see the possibility of a stable, peaceful and contemplative way of life. Harmony with nature, an ego like water, non-attachment with no clutching or punishing – it is a less noxious ideal than most of the ideals people have lived by.

How then does the Christian's selflessness differ from the sceptic's, and is it rational of me to go on pursuing it with so little prospect of success?

The sceptic gives his highest priority to maintaining his peace of mind. He withdraws from historical striving and from ecstatic love because they are both of them too risky and uncomfortable. Frankly, it is unwise to get involved. The Christian, by contrast, does not allocate so high a priority to peace of mind. Most fundamental in his scheme of things is the decision of faith in response to the call of Jesus. The act of renouncing an old order of things and receiving a new order becomes the leading *motif* in the Christian conception of existence. It means that he attempts to live by a continual active self-surrender and receptivity which generates both his social ethics and his personal ethics. 'I die daily' (I Cor. 15.31) is his watchword.

In social ethics this means that he is committed to history and to historical change, for he sees history as the theatre wherein spiritual development takes place. There actually is a slow and erratic but real historical development of human consciousness and spiritual individuality. As a Christian I must struggle historically to develop and intensify my own and other people's free individual consciousness. The chief requirement in Christian social ethics is the maximization of each individual's spiritual autonomy. But in order to advance in consciousness I have to learn to will inner and not just outer change, and *inner* change has to be willed by the 'I die daily' method. For example, one must renounce mean, exclusive and partisan forms of consciousness and move out to the larger and more universal consciousness of disinterestedness. One becomes more free as one becomes less egoistic and tribalistic. Yet it is very hard to do, and involves a kind of death, for *interest* whether personal, class, national or whatever, is a prodigiously strong and tenacious force.

Similarly in personal ethics the Christian seeks to die to and abjure the enslaving personal relationships that are characteristic of the old order of things, and to learn instead a non-domineering and non-manipulative kind of love, *agape*. If love can become disinterested then it will be possible to reconcile love with the other's freedom. We will love in a way that is not oppressively jealous and demanding but which actually liberates the other, making the other more autonomous and not less.

The 'I-die-daily' method of bringing about the historical advance of free consciousness and the reconciliation of love with freedom is bloodily painful and difficult. The historical record shows that it has too often degenerated into psychological perversity. Nevertheless when it does succeed it is the best. That is the only reason that can be given for pursuing it. If someone says, 'Why not settle for sceptical spirituality? You are more likely to achieve a modest degree of happiness along those lines, and sceptics do little harm, which is more than can be said for believers' – well, the only reply that can be made is that one must attempt the best.

Certainly there is not anything more fundamental than religious

commitment, in terms of which religious commitment can be justified. For religious commitment comes first of all. It creates one's
form of ethical personhood, which is why the doctrine of creation
so often comes first in theology. Religious commitment involves
my decision as to the way in which I insert myself into existence
or, to put it otherwise, the way in which I will to be present in the
world. In the past religion was doubtless many other things as
well, but today it is one's decision as to one's mode of presence in
existence. A particular way of relating oneself to existence is a
form of faith, and it is the choice of one's form of faith that sets
one up in existence as a moral agent by establishing the overall
framework within which morality operates. So faith is prior to
morality, for it determines the general shape of the moral life.

There are many forms of faith, each with an associated cluster
of characteristic values and virtues; but since the decision of faith
comes first – so much so as to constitute the form of our personhood – it is hard to imagine oneself making a reflective choice
between forms of faith from some standpoint anterior to any of
them. So it is hard to see what could count as a justification of the
fundamental religious commitment – except to say simply that one
must choose the best for its own sake.

Until the Enlightenment it seemed reasonable to believe that
one's religion had been revealed by God. It was 'objective' divine
truth. Usually people were not so crude as to suppose that the
thing revealed was a set of propositions. The intellectualist or
realist heresy is rather modern. What they typically thought had
been revealed was a law or a way, a form of faith and pattern of
religious existence. If the law or way was God-given it was obviously reasonable to follow it and to hold that by following it one
would attain final happiness.

It is clear by now that revelation-beliefs are mythological. They
are picturesque enforcers of the authority of the scriptures. Every
religion claims that its scriptures and its path to salvation have
come down from heaven, but what really happend is that the books
were written and the path was worked out by human beings. To
adapt a point Hume makes about miracles, in so far as each religion
makes out a case in support of its own revelation-claims the various
cases thus made are bound to cancel each other out.

A different kind of justification of religious endeavour was offered by Hegel. The whole universe is the expression of the striving
of Spirit towards self-actualization. So if asked, 'Why should we
struggle laboriously towards larger, freer, more universal and dis-

interested forms of consciousness?', then Hegel would answer, 'Because the inner striving of the whole world-process is in that direction.' But Hegel's doctrine has rather less in it than appears at first sight. *Geist* or Spirit appears not to be anything over and above all the individual human consciousnesses in which it is manifested, and in any case it still needs to be shown why we should swim with the current. Hegel says, 'My explanation of why you should strive for a higher form of consciousness is that the whole world-historical movement of *Geist* is in that direction.' We answer, 'Why go along with *Geist*?' Hegel replies, 'It is a religious duty' – which shows that he is still at the starting point, and has not advanced a single step towards a general justification of religious endeavour.

note + I suggest that the pursuit of the religious ideal needs no extraneous justification and cannot be given one. We pursue it because it is the best; disinterestedly, because it is disinterestedness. One must seek a higher purity and intensity of consciousness, because consciousness itself – and perhaps all biological life – is such a teleological striving. The human race as a whole makes some progress, and that is some consolation for the fact that I make so little.

10

FAITH AS AN ACT OF THE WILL

In prescientific culture religious language was multi-functional. It did several different jobs at once, describing what is the case, expressing a response to reality as thus understood and committing the believer to future religious obedience, and it worked in this many-sided way not through ignorance or inattention but because traditional religion springs from the deepest, most primal and archaic level of the mind, where distinctions that will later come to seem very important are as yet unknown. The archaic mind works by symbolization and its symbols are descriptive, expressive and action-guiding, all together.

In scientific culture this archaic unity is largely lost. Traces of it may survive in childhood, in dreams and in art, but in most of our sober waking life and especially when it is important to be precise and accurate we now use language in a much more differentiated way. The most important of the distinctions we have come to make is that between the scientific use of language and all the other non-scientific uses, for we have found that to gain our powerful bodies of scientific knowledge we must learn a special way of speaking, impersonal, dispassionate and value-neutral; a kind of language that has been specially designed to mean only one thing and to do only one job. The archaic use of language had been very rich. It meant many things at once, it did many jobs at once and it was evocative and ambiguous – like the language of art, which still remains closest to the archaic mind. But this richness and complexity is an utter muddle from the point of view of science. The experimental method demands a highly analytical turn of mind. The experimental subject and the control must differ in one respect only; all other variables must be detected and eliminated. In science everything depends upon precision, univocity and avoidance of ambiguity.

The method certainly works, for it has created the first really large, powerful, well-organized and intellectually-beautiful bodies of knowledge that human beings have ever had. But the linguistic specialization that we have had to learn has separated science, art and morality from each other and has left religion in particular in a very anomalous position. Traditional religion came up from a level of the mind deeper and older than the split between fact and value, and it quite unselfconsciously joined together hypothesis and obligation, talk about how the world is and talk about what we should do. It simply did not distinguish between given fact and moral requirement.

Science does so distinguish. It entrenches in our culture the ideas of the value-neutral state of affairs and the value-neutral use of language. It forces us to discriminate between those assertions about the world that are in principle publicly testable by standard procedures and those that are not. Once made, this is a fateful distinction that forever separates science from everything that – however estimable – is not science.

Some people try to resist the implications of this. They say, correctly, that facts are more dependent upon theories and less 'pure' than used to be thought. True: so we simply shift the emphasis from the value-neutral fact to the value-neutral theory. Others claim that science is more ideological than its orthodox apologists realize. But no amount of such talk can alter the evident fact that science is nowadays able to penetrate every culture in the world with equal ease. Properly applied by competent professionals, modern scientific medicine, agriculture and so forth work well enough to impress the local populace everywhere, whatever the local religion or ideology, whereas the power and authority of gods is evidently restricted to certain regions. The Virgin Mary may cure many people in Portugal but she is much less active in Libya, whereas vaccination and inoculation are observably beneficial – and equally beneficial – in both cultures, the local religion in the end making no difference at all.

Once all these points have been grasped it becomes clear that the scientific revolution forces a dilemma upon traditional religion: hypothesis or obligation?

By 'hypothesis?', I mean this question: 'In the new situation created by the rise of modern science, shall religious belief stake out a claim to be factual or descriptive in the new sense and according to the new standards that science has so brilliantly established?' Some say, Yes. As we remarked earlier, the eighteenth-century deists made a necessary attempt to define and defend a small body of universal and cross-culturally valid religious knowledge, but they are now generally agreed to have failed. Others who also answer yes take the view which in the course of my present argument I have variously labelled realism, intellectualism, or objectivism. This intellectualist view of religious truth thinks itself to have the monopoly of continuity with the tradition and all other virtues. But in my running battle against it I have put forward a number of counter-arguments. Realism is not traditional, because the tradition was prescientific and so could not have known anything of the chief task realism sets itself, namely that of meeting the novel standards of truth, objectivity and factuality set by science. In trying to live up to these new and deeply alien standards realism – as I have repeatedly pointed out – weakens itself as religion. William Paley (1743–1804), the author of *The Evidence of Christianity* (1794) and *Natural Theology* (1802), is an excellent example of a writer whose account of religion, under the influence of natural science, is so 'objectified' and propositional that it fails as an account of *religion*. Paley's God is so factual and his religion so worldly, so prudent and utilitarian that he has no room at all for the loftier religious virtues, such as the disinterestedness that I have stressed so much.

Modern realists – philosophers of religion, Vatican officials, conservative churchmen, orthodox agnostics – think of themselves as defenders of 'objectivity' and the traditional meaning of religious language. Paley shows where they go wrong. Paley is not at all traditional: nobody in the Bible, for example, thinks of religion in a way that even remotely resembles Paley.

I spoke of a dilemma forced upon modern religious belief by the fact-value split: hypothesis or obligation? The way of hypothesis struggles to claim that religious beliefs are something like scientific hypotheses and the result is a theology such as Paley's. At the level of meaning it is a poor interpretation of what religion is all about, and at the level of truth it is probably false anyway. Paley's God does not exist; though I have put the point more cautiously by saying that we do not have such overwhelming evidence that a Paleyan God exists as to be justified in committing our whole lives upon its reliability.

The other way is the way of obligation, a voluntarist interpretation of religion such as is espoused here. Religious faith is a free decision to bind religious obligations upon oneself and to commit oneself to the pursuit of religious values. The realists will point out that religious language in prescientific times undoubtedly did have a cosmological and descriptivist strain in it. Of course it did. Modern realism naturally appeals to and builds upon that observation, and I must admit that in so far as I am abandoning such claims as no longer defensible I am departing from tradition. In mitigation of this confessed heterodoxy, though, I plead that there is no merit in clinging to untruths. So far as the myths in Genesis 1–11 contain or imply factual assertions about how things are, those assertions are largely false. Many theologians say, 'Ah, yes: we know Genesis 1–11 is myth; but we do not actually believe the *myths*, we believe the underlying doctrines', but the doctrines were built on the presumption that those myths were revealed truths, so why go on affirming the doctrines when the myths will not sustain them any longer? (A parallel case is the way people cling to certain doctrines about Jesus long after modern gospel criticism has eroded the premises from which those doctrines were originally deduced.) Others defend Genesis by saying, 'Ah, yes, but there is profound truth in myths', but mythic truth is also split into two elements by the fact-value fork. The descriptive element in mythic truth, when separated out, proves to be false, and the value-element we preserve (insofar as it is indeed intrinsically valuable) not because it is in the myth, but for its own sake.

And is the realistic or cosmological element in religious belief quite so important as people say it is? I doubt it. Christianity began not as a cosmological religion but as a religion of redemption, and Jesus required not assent to metaphysical assertions but a moral decision for a new world. The Bible contains no propositional faith (that is, in the usage of the biblical writers 'faith' does not take, or only very rarely takes, a proposition as its object), and the Bible consistently understands 'the knowledge of God' in practical not speculative terms. Indeed the modern intellectualism which is so self-satisfied about its own traditional virtue is very close to the deadly heresy of Gnosticism, salvation by special esoteric knowledge. All those neo-conservative Christians who are so numerous today appear to identify 'being a sound Christian' with 'assenting to all the right propositions'. Having a strong faith is equated with scoring the maximum on a doctrinal check-list – and this on the part of people who sincerely believe that their own religion is biblical!

I have followed instead the path of those who say that religion is a matter of the will rather than the intellect. Faith is a virtue, not a means by which we gain esoteric information about occult entities. Faith is not theoretically cognitive and on the account I have given we do not have any reliable information about a world-transcending God at all. Faith is practical, a way of binding oneself. I impose the religious requirement upon myself and pledge myself to the pursuit of religious values. I choose my religion, all of it.

If I could have theoretical knowledge of God as a distinct object other than myself, including knowledge of what it is that God wills, and if these facts about God and God's will were in themselves sufficient to impose religious obligation upon me, then faith would be through-and-through heteronomous. I would be subject to an almighty will ruling me from without. How can such a heteronomous faith ever be the means whereby I become autonomous and fully-liberated spirit? It is impossible. This appears to be a conclusive religious argument against the objective existence of God. An objective God cannot save.

I therefore maintain that by the criterion of religious adequacy (or fitness to bring us to salvation) faith must be understood in a thoroughly voluntarist way and God in a thoroughly internalized and non-objective way.

As we have seen, modern science has very effectively separated the worlds of fact and value. The world of physical fact and theory is value-neutral; the world of value is non-factual and is posited by the will. The province of the intellect is the world of fact and theory; the province of the will is the world of value. So in relation to the world of value it seems that voluntarism is true; that is, it is the will that chooses goals, autonomously prescribing life's shape and direction. Thus we have a disjunction between the factual world that is acknowledged, and the world of value that is posited. To which of these worlds does religion belong? This is a dilemma that religion would have preferred to avoid. Intellectualism or voluntarism? The choice must be made: it is one or the other.

Intellectualism seems to identify religious faith with assent to a body of propositions. The interests of church authority, nostalgia for an obsolete world-view, and public dislike of religious change have all combined to make intellectualism very popular. Intellectualism is heteronomous, as we showed, and spiritually immature. It is very authoritarian because the more you see religious faith as assent to a set of propositions which are factual but not strictly empirically verifiable, the more you will be obliged to rely upon external authority to certify the truth of those propositions. So among Protestants, Catholics, Muslims and other groups we have in modern times seen faith becoming more heteronomous, authoritarian and immature. Most serious of all, this highly objectified conception of faith fails *as spirituality* and is in my belief at least partly responsible for the decline of religion. In the absence of strict proofs of theological propositions, intellectualism has no choice but to seek guarantees. It gradually reduces religion to infantile dependence upon paternal authority telling us what to think and what to do. Eventually spiritual freedom and the power of salvation are squeezed out altogether. Everybody knows it: authoritarian dogmatism kills freedom, and there is no power of salvation without freedom.

Yet voluntarism, in spite of its promise of maximal autonomy and free consciousness is, I have to confess, so unattractive to people that most have never heard of it and are not aware that it even exists as a religious possibility. So far as it ever gains a hearing, it is usually dismissed. In its lax Victorian Matthew Arnold form it will be reviled as vapid, and in its stringent Kierkegaardian form it is criticized for being too difficult for ordinary people. The voluntarist interpretation of faith can take many forms, and it is perhaps a fair complaint that it has never been really clearly expounded in any of them. I have tried here to be plain, but inevitably the plainer you are the more negative you sound, and voluntarism somehow continues to appear to be on the defensive in comparison with intellectualism. In seeking to overcome this chronic handicap I have used several specifically-religious arguments against intellectualism and for voluntarism.

I have just used an expression that needs to be defined: the 'specifically-religious' concern is the concern for salvation. I use the adjective to describe those things that directly bear upon our actual attainment of salvation. It is in this area of the specifically-religious interest in salvation that the voluntarist interpretation of faith is so greatly superior to its chief rival.

Yet voluntarism gains its religious superiority only at the price of being doctrinally very unorthodox, and most people remain so firmly wedded to intellectualism that they will scoff at the suggestion that their religion cannot become spiritually effective until they renounce their objectified theological beliefs. To clarify the case for voluntarism, then, let us investigate how far there can be in the voluntarist's practice of religion some return of objectivity. Kierkegaard, for example, claims that when inwardness reaches its maximum it proves to be objectivity again.[1] Kant, a strong voluntarist, is willing to concede a partial reinstatement of theological beliefs as moral postulates.[2] And you may well demand of me some account of what I make of prayer and worship.

Prayer and Worship

Beginning with prayer and worship I should say at once that, holding a voluntarist view of faith, I am not obliged to save all the phenomena. I do not have to find some kind of defence or reinterpretation of all present practices. The basic reason is that voluntarism is not so limited by the given as is intellectualism.

To see why, compare a moralist on the one hand with a spokesman or an interpreter on the other. These last two characters are limited by the given. The spokesman is hired by a group to present the activities of that group in as favourable a light as possible. It is not his business to admit errors but to make out the best case he can. His job is advocacy. As for the interpreter, I am thinking here of someone whose task it is, perhaps, to describe an exotic culture. He describes and explains, but he must not judge. His business is understanding. He and the spokesman are both of them theorists who seek to persuade us to see all the facts in a certain light. They have to do justice to *all* the facts, and in that sense are limited by the given.

The moralist is unlike these two characters. Ethics is normative, not descriptive, and the moralist must work out how things ought to be, what principles ought to be adopted, what judgments ought to be made.

Now on the voluntarist view, the theologian is more like the moralist than the interpreter, because faith cleaves to principles rather than to propositions. Religious allegiance is a free and practical choice, and the problem is to get the choice right. Since faith is an act of the will, not describing given facts about a higher order, but willing the arrival of a better order of things, theologians and philosophers of religion are talking about how things ought to be. The task is creatively to formulate true religious principles such as it is right to adopt, and to criticize and to repudiate wrong religious principles such as ought not to be adopted. So one must be a revisionist, not out of perversity of spirit but in the same way that a moralist must be a revisionist. One is declaring what ought to be, and not simply interpreting what is already, the case.

Many philosophers of religion are most reluctant to see this point and modestly decline to involve themselves with theological revision. They talk as if religious belief-systems were immutable. The idea is, I think, that such a belief-system makes very grand claims for itself. It purports to be revealed from a higher world, and to tell us about the acts and intentions of One who lives in that higher world. And if that is what a religious belief-system is, then one may ask about its credentials and consider whether to accept or reject those stupendous claims, but it seems presumptuous and rather silly to contemplate *revising* them. They are what they are. It is not our business to alter Christianity. We can talk about the meaning and the truths of its claims, but changing them is out of the question.

This widely-held view is, however, bare-faced intellectualism once again. It assumes that the essence of Christianity – the 'deposit of faith', as Catholics call it – consists in a specifiable set of unchanging theological assertions. Nothing can be done about them: they have always been the same and their meanings are clear and do not change. They are Christianity, revealed from heaven. We have only to add that the custody of this set of propositions is vested in the hierarchy, whose duty it is to give the final ruling in any disputes about the deposit of faith, and all speculative and revisionist religious thought are satisfactorily precluded. The only theology there can be is that psittacine recitation of the deposit of faith which in the church press is described approvingly as 'clear teaching'. Any actual thought is heresy. So intellectualism is, paradoxically, anti-intellectual. This view of the deposit of faith has come to be held very widely among Catholics and others, especially since the seventeenth century, but it is after all a relatively modern view. To avoid being hoodwinked we have to remember that the slogans of those who call themselves conservative, traditionalist, orthodox and so forth are often very recent coinages. Among Catholics, the traditionalists defend papal infallibility and some radicals question it. It all sounds as if (and the traditionalists naturally want it to sound as if) the infallibility of the Pope is one of those timeless truths that were always peacefully accepted in the church in the good old days before troublemakers began to rock the boat. Yet a moment's reflection will remind all concerned that on this issue, as on so many others, the radicals hold the old view and the conservatives are the upstarts. Nobody in his right mind can seriously claim that the teaching of Pope John Paul II is closer to the New Testament faith than the teaching of Professor Hans Küng. Maybe neither is close, but John Paul is certainly not closer.

The intellectualist view that Christian faith necessarily involves assent to a specifiable set of immutable propositions is false. If it were true then its truth ought to have been recognized from the beginnings of Christianity; but it was not.[3] On the contrary, the intellectualist thesis is itself a relatively modern formation, and one moreover that is quite unhistorical, for it is an evident fact that Christianity itself and also ideas as to what constitutes the essence of Christianity are both of them in continual historical change and have been different in every century.

So intellectualism is false and philosophers of religion have no need to be intimidated by it. Like morality, religious truth has to be creatively formulated and not just passively accepted from those who for whatever reason wish to wield religious power over us. Religion, or devotion, has almost nothing to do with the assent of the intellect to doctrinal propositions. Religious truth is practical. It has to be chosen and done, for it is a matter of the will.

There is then no reason to regard existing practice in matters of prayer and worship as if it were a sacrosanct totality, like holy orthodox tradition, within which it is forbidden to discriminate. On the contrary, some features of present practice may well turn out to be absurd, illogical or superstitious. If so, one should not seek to reinterpret them but should urge that they be discarded.

We find though that it is often hard to say at what point one should decide to give up reinterpreting a practice and instead urge its abandonment. A classic case is that of petitionary and intercessory prayer. For a long time now, theologians have been taking themes from the tradition and working them up in such a way as to hint that *we must answer our own prayers*. They say that it is superstitious to think we can manipulate divine power to bring about desired effects. Prayer is not magic. God acts through men and not apart from them. We should not resort to prayer out of indolence, asking God to help others and ourselves because we are too lazy to do anything about it for ourselves. What we pray for we must will with all our might, and we must be prepared to be ourselves the ones through whom God answers our prayers. Prayer must be closely tied to moral endeavour.[4]

So runs a very typical line of modern theological argument, and it is disturbing. For it sounds suspiciously as if the theologians (whether aware of it or not) are keeping themselves and their readers blindfolded, so that nobody quite becomes fully aware of the real drift of the argument. That, I am sorry to say, is the way it too often goes; in much theological argument the blind lead the blind and nobody knows he is blind. But we have chosen the way of full consciousness – inevitably, for what is the use of religion if it keeps you in the dark? So we try to admit consciously the drift of the theological argument in cases such as this. To say that 'God makes creatures make themselves' is to say that creatures make themselves; to say, 'God helps those who help themselves' is to say that we must help ourselves – and so on. In the present case, prayer is a way of opening ourselves to the requirement that we have laid upon ourselves and meditating upon the ideals and values to which we have committed ourselves. We seek strength to meet adversity, love to give to our neighbour, courage and determination to overcome sloth and depression, and the will to will our own inner change. In quiet recollection we seek simplicity and clarity of mind so that the forces of renewal can do their healing work in us. In several senses of the phrase, *we pray for ourselves* and we have to answer our own prayers, for it is superstition to suppose that our prayers will be answered apart from our own efforts.

Suppose we consider what believers today most readily pray for, and what degree of confidence they feel in the varying sorts and degrees of petition and intercession. What we find confirms our thesis, for people are most confident where their prayer is most closely linked with human action. Thus few doubt that it is right to pray for graces and blessings for oneself, because in this case one is in a position to answer one's own prayers. All believers also think it a good idea to pray for friends in adversity because this prayer also is self-answering. After they escape from their adversity, those we prayed for tell us that it was a great comfort to them to know that they had the support of our prayers. The prayer of the congregation was a ritual expression of love and support. Like support on the sportsfield, it has a valuable effect on morale. When we pray for friends in trouble we give them just that kind of support and they for their part are glad to know that they are receiving it.

What of less direct kinds of prayer? By praying for peace we strengthen the arm of those who work for peace, and when we pray for the relief of hunger overseas our prayer is linked with our efforts to raise money for the cause.

What about praying for a person's recovery from illness? Believers add the qualifying clause, 'If it be thy will', and do not regard prayers for the sick as any sort of substitute for the application of medical science. So what is the use of religious acts on behalf of the sick? The answer seems to be that they are ritual gestures, more like the sending of flowers and a get-well card than like the administration of a drug – and such ritual gestures are very important. Indeed, there is no clear cut-off point at which expressive-ritual acts stop and technical-instrumental operations start. Rather, there is a continuous spectrum, with the most measurably-effective acts that can be performed for the sick at one end and the least measurably-effective acts at the other end of the spectrum. The physician knows that his patients benefit from visits, touch, tokens of affection, religious ministrations, personal and emotional support – but he recognizes that the ways in which such acts are beneficial are not quantifiable. So I suggest that the believer's attitude to his own prayer for the sick is that it seems to be helpful and supportive but in a way that cannot be measured, and that this attitude is reasonable.

If we press the discussion further, we begin to extend prayer beyond the sphere of human mutual care and affection, and beyond the scope of the human will. We move into regions where believers do not and perhaps never really did suppose prayer to be objectively effective. The human response to natural phenomena such as drought or famine is a fit topic for prayer, but the occurrence or non-occurrence of the phenomena themselves is not a fit topic. It is noticeable that we do pray for people to pursue truth diligently, but we do not think it appropriate to pray for the finding of solutions to specific technical problems, presumably because *in themselves* the technical problems and solutions are non-ethical. There are some areas of technology today where a breakthrough could have enormous implications for human well-being, but even so nobody seems to be suggesting that they are a fit topic for prayer.

I conclude that almost all actual prayers are directly about people's relation to moral and spiritual values. The ways in which believers today have come to practise prayer are broadly consistent with a voluntarist view of faith. Prayer seems to be concerned with the human will, the human pursuit of or failure to pursue moral and religious values, and mutual human care and affection. Prayer is an exercise of faith and devotion. How far people used to think there 'literally' was an objective God, who controlled all events and who could be swayed by prayers to modify the course events would otherwise have taken, may be disputed; at any rate they seem not to think it now. They seem now to think that when we call on God we are using language symbolically and expressively. Talking to God most beautifully expresses our wish to be rid of our own wickedness, our desire for spiritual rebirth, our aspiration

He does leave behind him the essence of rel.

contradict himself

after various infinitely-precious moral and religious values, our sense of human solidarity, and – above all else – our sense that life is short and we are dust, that the religious standard is eternal and its demand upon us measurelessly great and awesome. We express reverence and gratitude towards the religious ideal, for in a world that is so often dispiritingly meretricious it is one thing that is of eternal and inexhaustible worth and beauty.

We all begin by thinking of the religious ideal that we commune with in prayer as if it were a real person. We do this because the human mind has so powerful a tendency – possibly connected with the bicameral anatomy of the brain – to imagine that it has an invisible companion. There are endless examples of the phenomenon: gods, guardian-spirits, daimons, ancestors, inner voices. Some are rather more secular figures, such as the dead spouses and parents who continue to accompany the bereaved, the genii and muses of artists, the invisible playmates of solitary children,[5] the heroes of adolescence and the voice of conscience. We are particularly apt to personify the ideal we live by, for it is authoritative over us, it makes us what we are and it judges, guides, summons and inspires us. God is the most exalted and powerful of all such personifications. But God is not an actually-existing individual person. God is a humanly-needed way of speaking generated by the impact of the religious demand and ideal upon us. In private prayer we gradually learn to dispense with the notion that we are conversing with another person. It is good to start at that point, but in time we realize that the other person is becoming a cosy fantasy which is religiously harmful. We come to see that it is bad religion to overpersonify the religious ideal.

In the light of these findings we can now return to the question from which we started, namely, do we wish to change present practice or is it sufficient to have somewhat reinterpreted it? The nuances are fine. Consider this sequence: I hope my friend Peter is happy; I think of him every day; I do it at a certain time of day; I say to nobody in particular, 'Let him be happy'; I say, 'O God, make Peter happy'. Why take this last step? The advantage of doing so is that I give formality, weight and seriousness of purpose to my care for Peter by binding it up with the moral and religious values that are most precious to me. Prayer to God for Peter brings the eternal into my relationship to him. It is much more substantial than, indeed it is spiritually different in kind from, mere good wishes, kindly thoughts and fond remembrances. What adds the

weight is that the formal calling to mind of Peter is done before
the eternal. He is linked with that which has eternal worth.

I do not suggest that Christian prayer should be so severely
expurgated as to be reduced to nothing but meditation upon our
duties. On the contrary, petition and intercession deserve to be
practised because individual persons and their relationships have
eternal significance within the Christian scheme of religious values,
and it is right that by the practice of prayer we should maintain
those values undiminished. The acid test is surely this: can we
continue to practice intercession and other kinds of prayer after
we have become fully conscious of what we are doing? I say we
can but we do need to be truly aware of what we are doing because
illusions are not good for us, and that means that one should
observe a certain restraint in thought and language. I suspect that
in fact most people already do this.

What of public worship? It is right that the language of public
worship should be both richly symbolic, because a widely shared
religious vocabularly has to be so, and archaic, because public
worship is so much concerned with historical continuity. Worship
is formal and expressive and it seems that the individual worshipper
is not expected to make his own, in his own present-day person,
all the words he sings, says and hears. After all, much of Christian
worship consists of Old Testament material that is vociferously
preoccupied with a society, a temple, a sacrificial system, an ark,
a covenant, a monarchy and so on which (so far as Christians are
concerned) all ceased to exist millennia ago! Yet the psalms in
particular have always been the most important single component
in Christian prayer. The original meaning and use of the psalms is
largely unknown but they certainly belonged to a milieu utterly
different from that of modern Christianity, so we do not even
know what it could be for a modern Christianity to say a psalm
with a full and scrupulous *ex animo* literalness and sincerity, meaning every word. Hence it is evident that nobody is or can be too
literalistic about the language of worship.

The difference today is that what has always been true of the
substantial Old Testament component in Christian worship has
now also become true of the specifically-Christian material derived
from the New Testament and the patristic period. This New Testament and patristic material includes the general shape of the
services and the organization of the church community, as well as
the Lord's Prayer, the New Testament, the sanctus, te deum, gloria
patri, gloria in excelsis, creeds and so on. It all belongs to a religious

system and world-view now as remote from moderns as the Old
Testament world has always been from Christians in general. To
put it bluntly, *classical Christianity is itself now our Old Testament*. As such, it is valuable to us in the way that the Old Testament
itself is also valuable. One does not have to be an ancient Jew in
order to be able to use the psalms with profit. Similarly, though
we have now evolved a long way from traditional Christianity, we
can still gain much from using its worship and steeping ourselves
in its language and imagery. Most of the religious beliefs are not
ours any more, but the specifically-religious values and many of
the moral values *are* still ours, so that in worship we rightly affirm
the historical continuity of the church and renew our allegiance to
our spiritual values at their source.

We have to use traditional Christianity in the same way as
Christianity itself has always used the Old Testament. In both cases
there is a great gulf but there is also continuity of spirit and
religious values. St Paul says that 'he is a Jew who is one inwardly',
meaning, it seems, that although the old external signs and organization of Jewishness are no longer important for salvation in quite
the way they used to be, nevertheless the spirit and inwardness of
Judaism have come through and have found fulfilment in the new
religious reality. Similarly, the only faith that is possible to us today
is a further internalization of traditional Christianity that preserves
its faith and values by taking them up into today's new spiritual
reality, the autonomous and post-theistic consciousness. But the
modern believer is just as much at home in and with traditional
Christianity as Christians in general are at home in and with the
Old Testament. Again putting it plainly, as one must, I celebrate
and take part in the eucharist just as straightforwardly and with
just as clear a conscience as all Christians sing psalms. When a
Christian sings a psalm he knows there is a religion-gap and a
culture-gap, but it does not worry him because he believes his faith
to be the legitimate successor of the faith of the psalmist. Similarly,
since the Englightenment there has developed a religion-gap and a
culture-gap between us and traditional Christianity, but we may
still be justified in using the old words if we can plausibly argue
that our present faith and spiritual values are the legitimate heirs
of the old.

After all, the rise of modern natural science and the industrial
revolution has been the greatest change in human affairs since
neolithic times. It is quite as big as a biblical change of
'dispensation'. So the religious change required in order to make

the transition to modernity will presumably be at least as great as the change between the Old and New Testaments.

What is our conclusion? The point of view sketched in this book is compatible with retaining much of the traditional ways in prayer and worship. Even after we have recognized that they are doctrinally obsolete, the old materials are often of splendid quality and still communicate genuine spiritual values. What is principally lacking is some recognition of the existence of other traditions and – still more important – some materials of equal quality which express a fully-conscious modern spirituality. These latter are entirely lacking as yet, because a fully modern Christianity scarcely yet exists. It lurks, I believe, in people's private opinions, but it has not yet won public recognition and acceptance.

However, by the same argument it has been made clear that our comparatively conservative attitude to prayer and worship does not imply a return of objectivity. It still appears that to permit a return of objectivity would be a betrayal of the distinctively modern spiritual achievement, the autonomous consciousness.

not true

Can Objectivity Return?

We have not yet found any return of objectivity, and we need to ask what such a return could possibly be. Certainly religious thought and imagery are deeply imbued with ideas of divine restitution after voluntary surrender. After the death comes the resurrection, after the loss the gain, after the struggle the victory, after the hunger the satisfaction, after the poverty the riches, after the darkness the light, after the affliction the reward. The religious life is hard but one is promised that it has a goal. It moves towards and it will attain a blessed consummation. We begin by seeking solitude, silence, nakedness, poverty, emptiness, forgetfulness, ignorance, and inner and outer detachment. We go on to suffer aching dissatisfaction, yearning, doubt, depression, bitter anxiety, barrenness . . . why do we endure all this? For the sake of a glorious fruition yet to come, which we naturally describe as a reversal of all the miseries we are presently enduring.

However, although for poetic purposes the loss and the gain are often described in a very precisely balanced way, we should not make the crude mistake of supposing that God pays us back in precisely the same coin that we first gave him:

Whatever, Lord, we give to Thee

> Repaid a thousandfold will be;
> Then gladly will we give to Thee,
> Who givest all.

[handwritten marginal note: "he has a literalist view of scripture"]

Imagine that the hymn-writer is meditating upon the soundness of an investment and say that verse with emphasis upon the word 'gladly', and the absurdity will become apparent. Why does there have to be such severe renunciation in the religious life? If in the end God proposes to restore to us several times over just the very things that we gave up, what was the use of all the loss and self-denial? The answer commonly given is that God is testing the disinterestedness of our love for him, as for example in the story of Abraham and Isaac. But if God says 'Give me a penny and I'll give you back tenpence later', what kind of test of disinterestedness is that?

Alternatively we might say that the purgative way is a kind of athletic training or military discipline. But this metaphor when pressed too hard also becomes objectionable. If in the end all the images are restored and everything is reaffirmed, what was the purpose of the strict training? Was it just to sharpen our perceptions? Was it no more than an appetizer, like a brisk walk before a big, big dinner?

It is clear that we must not interpret the imagery of loss and gain too literally. The resurrection is not an exact reversal of the crucifixion, and Jesus is not restored to just the same biological life that he had before his death. As a matter of fact, if the risen Jesus were to be restored to just the same physical life as he had had previously his crucifixion would lose most of its religious significance. It would be no more than an unfortunate mistake, now corrected and best forgotten. Everything would be as it was before, just as if the crucifixion had never happened.

Putting the point in the most general terms, religious teachings do indeed make extensive use of the themes of loss and gain, surrender and restitution, affliction and reward, but we should not suppose that what comes back is the same as what was given up. The way of purgation is more than just the first stage in a rather ludicrous transaction between man and God; it has substantial religious value in its own right. Life being what it is, death being what it is, human nature being what it is, we *ought* to follow the purgative way. It deserves to be followed for its own sake. It is a necessary training in self-knowledge and disinterestedness and as such is its own reward. You cannot without absurdity superadd a

reward for disinterestedness, and above all it is absurd to promise
to one who has learnt disinterestedness the reward of a large gift
of all the goods from which he has lately struggled free. It would
be like presenting a newly-reformed alcoholic with several cases of
malt whisky.

Applying this to our present topic, there cannot be a return of
objectivity in the sense of a coming back of the intellectualist or
realist notions that we have been trying to shake off. We needed
to free ourselves of them because they were bad, confusing ideas.
We do not need to be rewarded by getting them all back again.

What then can the return of objectivity be? Can it be anything
more than what we earlier called a picturesque reinforcer, a way
of encouraging people to persevere? It seems clear that there cannot
and there ought not to be any return of objectivity that nullifies
the spiritual gains made in the purgative way. The prophet Jeremiah once complained bitterly to God about what a hard time he
was having and how unjust life seemed to be. God replied tersely
that Jeremiah had suffered nothing yet:

If you have raced with men on foot, and they have wearied you,
    how will you compete with horses?
And if in a safe land you fall down,
    how will you do in the jungle of the Jordan?
                                            (Jer. 12.5, RSV)

That is admirably tough-minded and concedes nothing to human
weakness.

A classic and oft-quoted case of 'return' is that of the great
Spanish Carmelite mystic, St John of the Cross (1542–1591). When
we look at him, though, I think it becomes clear that St John does
not falter. Certainly the 'Doctor of Nothingness' (*el doctor de la
nada*) begins by being as severe as an Indian ascetic. He is not
pathologically self-punishing; he merely insists that heavenly as
well as earthly consolations must be eschewed. The one who ascends Mount Carmel must tread a very narrow path: *nada, nada,
nada* (nothing, nothing).[6] Can it be that, after the purgative way
is over, St John is changing his mind and claiming back again
everything that he had earlier renounced?

I do not think so. The love-unions take place by night, and it is
St John's consistent teaching that God remains 'dark night' to the
soul in this life. Furthermore, his language in the prose writings is
throughout regulative and not speculative in meaning. That is, he
gives only spiritual directions, rules and instructions: he does not

give a philosophy of God, nor a theory of man's knowledge of
God, nor the intellectualist's type of descriptive discourse about
God. His teaching has no informational content.

Here is an anecdote: I have more than once set philosophy of
religion students to study *The Ascent of Mount Carmel* and *The
Dark Night of the Soul*. 'After all,' I say, 'you want to know about
God, and St John of the Cross is the best. Admittedly, he is not a
philosopher but a mystic. Nevertheless, if man can know God,
John did. Let's look at him.' Back come the students, irritable and
disappointed: 'There's nothing there,' they complain. 'That's it!',
I say, 'That's it!'

John of the Cross is a voluntarist. His teaching, as it should be,
really is spiritual direction and not divine description. As for the
love poems, they really are *poems*, lyric expressions of the religious
ardour which keeps one tramping on the purgative way, and not
descriptions of an altogether different scheme of things which
comes into effect after the purgative way is over and done with.

What then of objectivity? There are various as-ifs in the religious
life. It is as if faith is objectively oriented towards an unknowable
transcendent. It is often as if in the spiritual life we have dealings
with a personal God. And there are many more such as-ifs, but
they are all mere adjuncts to faith, not independent powers. Only
faith can save and faith is an affair of the will, so objectivity comes
only insofar as faith by its own endeavours actualizes the good
that it wills.

models past historical figures

11

THE JUSTIFICATION OF FAITH

What sort of justification is appropriate for religious faith? The answer depends upon what religious beliefs are taken to be. On the realist or intellectualist view they are picturesque metaphysical claims, quasi-factual tenets about beings and activities which are somehow beyond the bounds of sense and therefore hard to detect by normal empirical means. But this theory has the disadvantage of appearing to put religious beliefs into the same basket as occultist, spiritualist and paranormal beliefs – beliefs that we usually describe as superstitious and irreligious precisely because they lack religious seriousness. They do not make the peculiarly comprehensive and searching demand upon our whole lives and our inmost hearts that is characteristic of religion. So how can religious beliefs be held to resemble them? A religious belief cannot be merely a superstition which happens to be true, for all kinds of superstitions find themselves being believed true without thereby acquiring any religious weight and seriousness. A superstition gratifies our appetite for hidden knowledge, for wonders, for power or magical protection, but it does not make the religious kind of claim upon us.

Nevertheless, many people do hold that faith rests upon supranaturalist assertions. They hold it so firmly that they cordially approve of the official persecution of theologians who try – ever so gently – to wean them away from their dependency on such ideas. On the realist view, religious faith is rational and justified if and only if a certain set of such supranaturalist beliefs is true. To justify faith, you must justify those beliefs.

The alternative view of faith that I have been describing has at least the merit of entirely disavowing such ideas and avoiding their company. I do not claim that there is any supernatural being or realm or activity nor that there is any part of us that will survive our deaths. Instead I see faith as a free decision to impose the religious requirement upon myself and to commit myself to the pursuit of a group of religious values. Religious belief is religious allegiance expressed in symbolic language. Oddly enough, belief originally *was* allegiance, for to believe simply meant 'to hold dear'. What I believe is that to which I profess loyalty and which I take for my guide.

There is much more overlap between the religions in this area of spirituality and values than there is in the realm of doctrine. Historically, doctrine has tended to become ideology and has been used to exclude the heretic and to separate believer from infidel. In so far as this use of doctrine has been emphasized, the religions have inevitably come to seem closed, mutually-exclusive and ir-reconcilable ideological blocs. Not surprisingly, people then begin to see religion in general as an ugly, obscurantist and divisive force in human affairs.

On our voluntarist view of faith a much more congenial picture emerges. The major religious traditions need not be considered as excluding each other. None is 'pure', for history tells that they have all been unashamed borrowers at one time or another in their pasts. They are complex, many-dimensioned traditions of faith, spirituality and values to live by, and they overlap each other. Separation is irrational in our world. Why not move freely among them? No doubt every one of us belongs primarily to one tradition, but there is no reason why we should not borrow from the others. Eclecticism is no sin. For example, like many other Westerners I am a Christian who much admires some elements within Buddhism and Judaism. Moreover, within the Christian tradition itself I am selective, as is everyone else. Again, why not? Nowadays we are very much aware of the varieties of individual personality and religious outlook. So far as world-view, spirituality and values are concerned everyone in our culture now puts together a personal package. Such liberty and variety need not be corrupt or confusing. It can be enriching, provided we each strive in our own way to make a religiously-valuable and coherent whole of our lives. We already have such pluralism in art and in morality, and we accept that it is in those domains a good thing. Now is the time to accept that the same principles hold in the case of religion. The age of religious chauvinism and totalitarianism is over: let the age of religious free expression begin!

Does this mean that in the sphere of religion anything goes, and that no general justification of religion is either desirable or possible?

No it does not: the case is closely related to that of morality, in several ways. First, although there are many ways of being moral and forms of moral life there are certain criteria that any morality must satisfy to merit the name – and they are rather stringent. Similarly there are many ways of being religious and forms of religious life, but there are certain criteria that any religious life must satisfy to merit the name – and they are stringent. In both cases there is an inner core which is stringent – in morality concerned with the form of one's doing and willing, in religion with the form of one's relation to existence – but around that core there is great freedom and possibility of variety. Secondly, morality and religion resemble each other in the following way: in each case a very nominal allegiance to the institution is socially more or less obligatory so that, for example, even unbelievers find themselves becoming involved with Christmas, monogamy, funerals and the like; but in each case also there are those who urge us not to be satisfied with merely nominal and passive participation in these great institutions. They say we should become much more personally and existentially involved. The justification of religion is therefore linked with and resembles the justification of morality. The issue is not one of descriptive truth, but of the depth of one's concern. We answer the questions, 'Why should I be moral?' and 'Why should I be religious?' by showing why it is important not to stop at the merely passive and minimal acknowledgment of these dimensions of life which is all that most people seem able to manage. We seek to show how greatly it matters to the existing individual subject that he should take both morality and religion with the utmost seriousness, and to this end one of the key things that we do in each case is try to expose the character and claims of the central requirement. Once it is clearly recognized, the requirement pulls us with the same kind of authority as an artistic vocation. Its transcendent claim upon us is that it is undeniably our immanent spiritual fulfilment. It is a way we must walk in.

Justifying religious commitment is thus very like and closely related to justifying moral seriousness. But does religion as here understood really differ from morality *at all*?

Put it this way: What does a morally serious person lack, that he should be asked to be religious as well? Is religious commitment over and above moral commitment so good a thing after all? For as we have seen, religious commitment is very demanding and people's success in attaining religious goals is very moderate. According to Christians, 'All have sinned' and nobody but Christ has adequately fulfilled the religious requirement. Other traditions may put it somewhat differently, saying perhaps that few reach the religious ideal or that it takes many lifetimes to attain it, but at any rate there is unanimity that the ideal is very difficult. Why attempt it at all? Might it not be argued that religion is an *ignis fatuus* and therefore morally damaging? In terms of Arthurian myth, it was perhaps the quest for the Grail that destroyed the Round Table. Only Galahad, Percival and Bors, the three best, achieved it and the remainder were badly damaged by their failure. After the Grail quest somehow things began to fall apart. So why superadd the religious realm beyond the moral? It seems that we need some explanation and justification of the additional claim of the peculiarly religious kind of commitment.

The answer is not a comfortable one. Essentially it consists in a most awkward paradox that has to be approached cautiously.

The first step is the religious claim and insight that holiness comes first: goodness presupposes holiness. Holiness is not an ideal limit at the far end of the moral life, but its necessary basis.

The insight here has been expressed in many different ways. Religion is shown to precede morality by ritual, which is much concerned with beginnings. Religious ritual sets up the moral framework within which one conducts one's life, or a stage in one's life, or a new relationship, or a new situation, enterprise or institution. Mythologically, God is pictured as ordaining the moral law. Protestant doctrine says that no good works can be done before justification, because a radical change in the religious status of the self has to have taken place before true morality can even become possible. Finally, Kant in his moral philosophy recognizes that to act well we must act as if we were already holy. Indeed, Kant, with his customary strength of mind, has the full paradox: the habitual exercise of the good will is the only route by which we can gradually approximate to holiness, and yet in a sense the good will already presupposes the holy will.

For it is an essential feature of the moral requirement that in morality one must be rational, that is, consistent and impartial. One should not respect persons, for one should not discriminate morally except for morally relevant and acceptable reasons. There must be no favouritism, no making of exceptions on one's own or anyone else's behalf. Nowadays it is unpopular to express the requirement of morality in the form of a set of universal and unconditionally-binding laws, because people suspect law-morality of being heteronomous, but such a way of teaching morality did have the great advantage of making it crystal-clear that moral judgment that deserves the name has to be consistent, impartial and capable of being made the general rule. There are a few other qualities that moral action and judgment must have, the most important being sincerity, authenticity or integrity – whatever is the opposite of pretence and hypocrisy. You must identify yourself with your act and put your heart into it, for any doubts about your self-identification with your own action are morally fatal. And that is enough to go on, for the moment. The point is – the moral requirement is so stringent that who but a saint can meet it?

We are liable to have an inflated idea of our own capacities in this regard, because we are so good at being objectively and impartially rational in certain restricted domains such as natural science, or the exercise of some bureaucratic function. In a restricted domain it is easy to be disinterestedly rational, so easy that we may not see that where one's whole life is concerned judgment and action that meet the moral requirement are extremely difficult, so difficult indeed that they can only spring from the consciousness of a saint, a consciousness that is universal and disinterested and that without any distortion or mixture of motives rationally loves the good for its own sake.

There are two points here. The first is that morality depends on consciousness, the range of moral possibilities open to us depending upon the form of life in which we participate and the range of ways of being a person that it makes available to us. The second is that actual human nature is so mixed and actual social orders are so distorting that we do not find and cannot expect to find among real people the purity of heart and universal, undistorted disinterestedness that morality requires.

Morality depends upon consciousness, which in turn is dependent upon the actual social order and form of life in which one participates. For example, if the social milieu does not allow me to come anywhere near to autonomy but keeps my consciousness at a relatively undifferentiated tribal level, then the only morality available to me will be a custom-based tribal kind of morality dictating to me the done thing for a member of my group who is in my position.

Again, suppose I am a low-ranking person in a class society. It is notorious that my morality will tend to be class-determined because my consciousness will tend to be class-determined. In a class society lower-ranking people are like minors compared with senior, higher-ranking people. So if we descend the social ladder we find ourselves regressing into an adolescent world. Men call themselves 'the boys' or 'the lads'. One has to take orders a good deal. Consciousness is more heteronomous, morality more a matter of command and obedience, childrearing more authoritarian and social attitudes stricter and more extra-punitive.

Thus we are made alarmingly and distressingly aware of the way class influences consciousness and morality, though one must not speak deterministically, for nowadays universal literacy and their perception in the new communication-media of other life-possibilities gives everyone at least a chance of liberation. Even in the most cruelly closed and manipulated societies word gets round, and the moment that the pressure is eased a little voices are raised calling out for autonomy and democracy, as they were recently in China. People snatch at the hope of a higher possibility as soon as they hear of it. They have marvellous antennae for detecting chances of spiritual emancipation.

In class society it is everyone who suffers spiritually and not only the lower-ranking people. For the dominant group, having more access to education and culture, will on the whole tend to enjoy a relatively more autonomous consciousness but in so far as they are thus more aware they must recognize the price that others have paid so that they, the ruling group, can enjoy their comparative emancipation. In so far as they are morally aware they must see this spiritual inequality as morally objectionable. Inequality in such relatively insignificant matters as wealth, power, longevity and the like might possibly be justified as being in the best interests of all – perhaps even in the best interests of the disadvantaged, as John Rawls requires.[1] But it is hard to see what in the world or out of it could ever justify the imparity of consciousness that seems inseparable from class society. It is a peculiarly hopeless and desperate kind of inequality, made even more objectionable when religious heteronomy is cynically imposed in order to sustain it.

In a class society therefore it seems that few can attain spiritual fulfilment with moral integrity except by dropping out or in some other such extraordinary way, and even then the moral ambiguity is plainly not entirely removed for you need to be relatively advantaged to be able even to perceive the possibility of such a remedy. Fully-developed spirituality ought to be for all, and not just for some at the expense of others as in Plato's *Republic*. Hence the great religions – or at least Judaism, Christianity, Islam and Buddhism – all cherish the ideal of a primitive brotherhood of equals.

Forms of morality then are linked with forms of consciousness (which are themselves, by the way, modes of relation to existence). We will be fully capable moral agents only when we have become spirit, that is, when we have a universal, disinterested, rational and autonomous consciousness that loves the good for its own sake. Such a consciousness is not limited or deformed by nationalism, class, religious group, egoism or any kind of faction or fearfulness. It is the consciousness of a saint, such as can only become the norm in a classless society of fully-emancipated individuals.

Since, as we saw earlier, the reality of God is the effectiveness of the religious ideal, the perfect society in which the ideal is fully effective is the kingdom of God. Whether or not it is attainable in history by human endeavour has been a highly contentious question, and it is contentious because of our paradox. We will not have complete moral integrity until there is such a society, so we must certainly strive for it; but how can we strive effectively? Surely our efforts to achieve such a society, if they are to be effective, require and presuppose the moral integrity that we will not have until there is such a society?

Put it in individual terms: I do not like myself and I wish I were pure in heart. How can I become pure in heart? – I have to will it. And how do I have to will it? – wholeheartedly and with a pure heart! As the teacher without authority tells us, 'Purity of heart is to will one thing', and what can there be that more obviously requires utter singleness of purpose than the attainment of purity of heart itself? So I must be pure in heart if I am to attain purity of heart!

Doubtless influenced by Lutheran dogmatic theology and its doctrine of imputed righteousness, Kant tried to solve the paradox by claiming that we can consistently act *as if* our wills were holy. In this way he tried to do justice both to the point that we need a holy will in order to get off to a sound start in the moral life and to the point that there cannot be any other way to attain that holiness except by the sustained and habitual practice of virtue. We have to begin by acting as if we were holy and gradually we will become so.

A post-Freudian generation may well be sceptical about this path to holiness, but let us give Kant a little more space to develop his argument.

Human beings as they are do not will only the good but are subject to, and may yield to, many other pressures – particular desires, impulses and temptations. A holy will is a will not subject to such other pressures, not tempted in any way, and so loving and doing the good without any sense of conflict or even of obligation. A holy will is not inwardly divided nor in even the most tenuous sense heteronomously controlled, for there is no gap at all between it and the ideal it expresses in its acts.

Kant duly acknowledges both the mixed character of actual human nature and the exalted transcendent purity of the moral ideal. We are not holy, but we know we ought to be holy. How can it be done? – How else but by moral striving after holiness? However, since moral action is action upon a principle purely for the sake of that principle, moral action itself seems to presuppose the very inner integrity and disinterestedness that we do not yet have and are striving after. It seems that only moral striving can lead us to holiness, but only if we are already holy and pure in heart can we perform truly moral actions.

Kant answers that we are able to act as if our will were already holy. Though we have sensuous inclinations that can lead us astray, we are beings who are basically rational and we are capable of becoming progressively more purely rational. (On Kant's view, holiness is the fullest realization of practical rationality.) We have to do it by constantly acting as if we were more purely rational than as yet we really are.

To support this claim, Kant produces a strange metaphysical theory of human nature which involves a sharp distinction between the empirical and the purely rational aspects of the self. Since the theory is generally agreed to fail, and since it gets even Kant himself into considerable difficulties, there is no need to trouble ourselves further with it here. It fails, and we are left with the obvious commonsense objections. I know my own motives are always horribly mixed and murky, you know yours are, and all the evidence suggest that everyone else is the same – including those we most admire and including even those who are reckoned to be saints. It seems very doubtful whether habitual virtuous action does in fact change the basic constitution of human nature in the sense required. Ecclesiastical biography and hagiography have only recently begun to be more truthful, but they surely confirm that human nature is what it is and human motives are what they are, even in the case of saints – though we need not and do not admire and revere them any the less for that. Kant's theory of the way to

holiness is surely falsified by the facts. People are not like that. It
will not work.

Kant's solution thus appears to fail. He thought in terms of a
smooth, continuous transition from the moral to the religious. For
him the religious was nothing but the fullest development of the
moral, and he saw no reason why we should not be able quietly
and progressively to phase holiness into the moral life. He knew
that human nature is wicked but was convinced that practical
reason must be able to overcome that wickedness.

Unfortunately, it seems that the more seriously one is concerned
with motives in ethics and the more one searches the heart the
more one becomes lost in a thicket, enmeshed by evil and moral
ambiguity, trapped in existence and caught in the old predicament
that Luther calls the bondage of the will. Where shall we find the
singleness of will with which we must will to become pure in heart?
Until we have a morally better world, how shall we get the moral
integrity we shall need if we are truly to make a better world
without ourselves sowing the seeds of destruction in our work?

Equally discouraging is the issue of innocence and experience.
Those who are most highly engaged with life, most active and fully
conscious, we think of as having inevitably lost their innocence.
They are in varying degrees unavoidably compromised, sceptical
and worn. They are battered by life and their faces look lived-in.
How can such people ever become innocent and pure in heart
again?

At the other extreme there are the genuine innocents. The words
innocent, simple, natural all have the idiomatic meaning of half-
witted. Is it not somewhat depressing that those we call Christ-
figures are so clearly the weak, the fools, the victims, the butts,
those who are always on the receiving end and who never hurt a
fly because they are too weak to hurt anything? It is not the
assumption that the Christ-figure is a victim that is troubling, so
much as the assumption that he is so weak-minded as to be incapable of any decisive action. He does not become a victim through
cruelty, injustice or tragedy; he is a born victim through his own
ineffectuality and passivity.

In Western European languages the adjective *honest* has over-
tones of rustic simplicity and very moderate intelligence. An honest
man is a bumpkin. By contrast, consider the use of *knowing* and
its close relative *cunning* to mean sharp, flashy, wide-awake, quick
on the uptake, and shrewd with overtones of slyness, dissimulation
and deceit. How infallibly in the European towns do we oppose

intelligence and virtue as mutually incompatible! In a culture that thinks in such terms, the saint has no option but to be a hysterical half-wit and religious recluse. Spirituality suffers the extraordinary debasement of being reduced to sentimental pietism and masochism, as in Baroque piety. Saints must be freaks where there is such a strong tradition of moral scepticism, unable to see how a high degree of moral virtue can possibly exist in a person of full intelligence who is actively engaged with life. Yet surely the moral predicament that creates the scepticism also cries out for a more authentic religious deliverance?

Such lines of thought suggest the answer to the question we began with, of why there needs to be a specifically religious concern and commitment over and above the moral. Kant tended to make of the religious, holiness, simply an extrapolation of the moral. But there cannot be an easy transition from morality to religion. Our experience of moral ambiguity, corruption, paradox, deadlock is too sombre. Religion is concerned with death and rebirth, with a change in our relation to existence. Religion is about victory over evil. We turn to religion not because we seek ratification of our present morality and warm congratulations on our progress to date, but because in an evil world we need a discipline of transcendence and a path to deliverance. The religious requirement as we have described it is that way of transcendence, and the other heavenly world that we seek from religion is simply a regenerated self in a new relation to this world.

A morality that seriously concerns itself with motives and with psychology is inevitably led in the direction of religion. To avoid this conclusion, some would urge us to turn completely away from motives and intentions towards a morality that concerns itself only with the observable objective consequences of actions, namely utilitarianism. At first we seem to come out into clearer and larger air. It is a relief to escape from the confessional and the couch, for is there not after all something rather overheated, stifling and pornographic about psychology, obsessive self-examination and internalized piety? The utilitarians with their robust clear-headed concern for the public good seem admirably secular and sober.

Then doubts set in. Utilitarianism puts every human transaction of any kind whatever into one or the other of only two pigeon holes; it must be either a benefit or an injury. Every human relationship is either a relation between a benefactor and a beneficiary or a relation between a malefactor and a victim. Classification under these two headings is claimed to be exhaustive and to include everything of moral significance in human life. This is a clear absurdity. For one thing, psychology cannot be wholly eliminated: the benefits and injuries, pleasures and pains have to be realized in consciousness, and a distinction has to be drawn between the intended and the actual consequences of acts. At these two points and at others psychology, and therefore all that murkiness and ambiguity, will come creeping back in. For another thing, the utilitarian challenge to the indolence of habit and privilege – 'Just how much good does it do?' – works very well and is very stimulating in an environment where the basic framework-questions have been settled and are not in doubt. But if they are in doubt, it cannot answer them. It cannot of itself tell us whose pleasures and pains are to be taken into the reckoning, what things are pleasurable or painful and why, or what is to be done about the variability and malleability of human nature. So utilitarianism is a shrewd polemical move in ethics, but it can no more be a complete ethical theory than its counterpart, the verification principle, can be a complete theory of knowledge.

In conclusion, then, we return to the question of consciousness and to the particular kind of emancipation or transformation of consciousness with which religion is concerned. What is it, and does it work?

Historically, the true function of doctrine was to give guidance on this point. For a system of doctrine is a Jungian dream, a coded message about what we are to become. The meaning of religious doctrine is essentially ascetical and regulative; that is, it is a guide to the spiritual life. In symbolic language it shows what religion is concerned with.

Did the theologians of the past really suppose that in building up doctrinal systems they were describing the cosmos on the grandest scale? It is hard to say, but if they did they were wrong. On the descriptive side we now have modern astronomy and other sciences, which give a quite different and far superior account. As a sketch-plan and outline history of the cosmos – if that was indeed what it purported to be – traditional religious doctrine was very primitive and is now entirely redundant. But in the second place, what is really striking is how little this descriptive redundancy worries modern believers. Without any prompting, without even thinking about it, they now use many traditional doctrinal statements purely regulatively. For example, in current preaching and religious debate the creation-doctrine is called upon in the course of discussion about the ethics of the environment, property, sex and so forth. It is invoked to guide the course of moral debate, and this practical, decision-guiding use is now the only use that is made of the creation-doctrine. People do not dream of telling any more the sort of quaint creation-story that Milton tells in Book VII of *Paradise Lost*, and they do not seem to notice that anything has been lost. All the indications are that the regulative use of the symbol of creation was always more important than its alleged descriptive content. At least, if there was once an important descriptive element in the doctrine it is now lost, but the loss seems not to matter and the ethical use of the idea of creation continues unaffected.

This is encouraging. It is well known that most believers dislike and reject the idea of demythologizing religious doctrine. They feel it is too impious, too sceptical and too big a break with tradition. Yet when they are off their guard they are doing it all the time.

To demythologize successfully (and again people probably know this without being told) we need to bear in mind some of the main features of the mythological representation of spiritual realities. The first is obvious: *myth projects*, representing elements in consciousness and phases of the spiritual life as beings, events and regions in an imaginary primal or heavenly world. Secondly *myth projects back into the past*, representing that after which we aspire as a primal reality from which we have come. We are for example urged to pursue the religious ideal by being told that we were at first made in the image of God. Thirdly *myth explains from above*, whereas modern ways of thinking explain from below. In atomistic, analytical and evolutionary thought we tend to see all complex realities as having been built up by stages over a long period from simpler predecessors: indeed we now see every social institution, ourselves, and the entire cosmos in this way. In mythological thinking, by contrast, everything is seen in its relation to the ideal order, the world-view is constructed from the top downwards, and present reality is put into perspective by being seen as having declined from the primal perfection. The value of seeing things this way round is that it directs us to think, not what a long way we have come, but by what a long way we fall short of the ideal.

A good story helps to fix in our minds this feature of myth: the Masai women tell a tale to explain why they have no animals of their own but must look after their men's livestock. Originally, they say, women did have their own animals; giraffe, gazelle and all the rest of the creatures now thought of as wild. But the women were lazy and failed to rise early enough in the morning. Impatient to be fed, their livestock escaped. Now women have no beasts of their own and are obliged to serve men.

The assumption in the story is that a normal, unproblematic animal is a domesticated animal. What needs explaining is how some animals have come to be wild. Again we notice that mythological thinking is almost the exact opposite of scientific thinking.

In the Masai story the present unhappy state of affairs, with animals wild and women subject to men, is contrasted with the good old days when those animals belonged to the women who were thus independently wealthy. All over the world we find these stories of the fall of woman, because the subjection of women is very widely thought to be strange and anomalous, so that it needs some explanation and/or justification. Woman's present state is contrasted with her original equality or even, in some cases, superiority.

So, fourthly, *myth reverses and contrasts*. That is, it helps us to come to terms with the way things are by postulating another time when things were either the opposite way round or at least not as they are now. And this era when things were otherwise may be projected into the future as well as being set in the past, which gives us a fifth point, namely that *myth is cyclical*. In biblical terms, there is a future age of gold as well as a past. God may seem chilly and remote to believers today but there was a time in the past when he was close and powerful to save, and he has promised that there will come another such time in the future. Both Jewish and Christian liturgy and faith were upborne by memory and hope; solemn remembrance of the mythic mighty acts of God in the past and ardent expectation of a good time yet to come. The thought of better times past and future encourages us in the belief that the religious ideal is ultimately attainable, even though it may seem to be well-nigh impossible under present conditions.

How is the ideal to be attained? Again there is a striking and amusing contrast with scientific thought. In science, theory has to be the attentive, obedient and completely pliable slave of fact because experimentally-established fact has the power of life and death over theory. In myth it is the other way round, for *in myth the empirical ought to conform itself to the ideal* and fact grows into theory. Myth presents us with grand archetypes, standard patterns for us to grow into and conform ourselves to. The death and resurrection of Christ is such an archetype. It is not just a descriptive theory of how the spiritual life does work, but rather a normative pattern to which we ought to conform ourselves.

Finally, *myth is prolix*. Scientific explanation aims at simplicity, economy and rational consistency, but traditional thought abhors a vacuum, loves elaboration and hates to throw anything away. Thus in Christianity the ideal world of religion appears three times over, spaced widely apart and in very different guises. Set in the prehistoric past, Eden presents a delectable vision of harmony with nature, innocence and fertility. The prophet Isaiah can also imagine its being restored in the future (Isa. 11). Secondly, there is the mystical heaven of union with God for the soul after death, and finally there is the kingdom of God, an ideal future society on earth. Curiously, it does not figure in Christian art, but it has become more important since the Reformation.

It may seem odd to have three quite different visions of the paradisal world, one concerned with nature and set in the mythic past, one concerned with religious mysticism and set in the mythic world above, and one concerned with society and set in the mythic future. How strange; why not try to be more consistent and synthesize them in one location? But it cannot be done. Each bears witness to important values, none may be discarded, and the fact that they are so disparate is a warning that none of them is to be understood descriptively. There was no Eden, but the image of Eden in art says something beautiful about sex, fertility and nature. There is no upper world, but the image of heaven above says something about the rewards of striving after purity of heart and a deeper religious inwardness and non-attachment. There will not be any future kingdom of God on earth, but the symbol tells that we should not withdraw from temporality and society, for the religious ideal requires realization in time, in history, in society. The Christian does not, like the Muslim, pretend he can actually set up an ideal theocracy on earth, but nor does he join the Indian who fails to recognize any such ideal at all. Instead he prays, 'thy kingdom come,' and the prayer together with the faith that inspires it is, precisely, regulative. Its function is to govern action and aspiration.

Granted these general features of mythical thinking, we can begin to see why Christian mythology (or doctrine, as it is often called) takes the form it does. God the Father represents to us the religious requirement itself, eternal, unchangeable and all-powerful. He creates us as beings who can become spirit. Union with him who is pure transcendent consciousness, universal and sovereign over nature, is our destiny. Jesus, the brilliant Jewish teacher of the religious requirement, is made in Christian mythology into its exemplary fulfiller. He becomes a heavenly figure who moves in a great mythic circle out from God into the world of time and change where he is archetypally obedient, a martyr, and is then raised to eternal life and returns to his original heavenly glory. He has thus established a bridgehead of salvation in the world of fact, and the religious community grows out of him and continually reaffirms its union with him. This union of believers with Jesus and of Jesus with God is brought about by the divine Spirit, for spirituality, a higher degree of consciousness, *is* divine. Becoming spirit is always like receiving a gracious gift, for nobody can clearly imagine a higher degree of consciousness than he has − otherwise, he would already have it − so that progress in spirituality towards a more intense and liberated consciousness has to be received as divine grace.

Along these lines we can begin to see how Christian doctrine unfolds as a grand, mythicized expression of Christian values and spirituality. And if so, you may well ask, 'Why demythologize? If everything is there in the doctrine, the mythology, the art and the liturgy, why trouble to decode it? Surely a decoding of Christianity, like an interpretation of a poem, is something only needed by academics, poor creatures who live at second-hand?'

Certainly I must not take up the challenge to rehabilitate either academics in general or theologians in particular, for it would be a waste of breath. But there are a few things to be said in defence of our argument as a whole.

The first and most important is that religion is dying, slowly fading away from the world, its internal qualitative decline being more disturbing than the declines either in the power of religious institutions or in the proportion of people who are believers. Why is this happening? Our diagnosis sees it as a by-product of the accelerating growth of secular knowledge since the later middle ages. Struggling to emulate the new sciences and to maintain her social authority, the church claimed that her beliefs comprised a system of quasi-factual knowledge higher, more certain and more authoritative than the knowledge obtained by the secular sciences. This is intellectualism, and it has tended to grow more extreme and more naive in spite of many protests. Intellectualism is bad religion for it represents a loss of understanding by the church of her own faith, and it was a disaster in external relations for it led faith into futile conflicts with secular knowledge in which it has been decisively defeated every time. The struggle against intellectualism is a step towards recovery.

Christianity on an intellectualist interpretation is regressive in that it leads one back into a primitive and childish world-view, and it is heteronomous in that it projects the objects of religious concern as real beings, powers, influences etc., to which one becomes subject. Now in the seventeenth century intellectualism was very strong in the church: consider a man like Bossuet, for example. Yet in the same period there was immense confidence and pride in *autonomous* human reason. The result was that some time around the year 1700 – give or take a generation either way – a distastrous split took place.[2] The leading edge of European spiritual development broke away from Christianity, and the gap has been slowly widening ever since. The leading edge with its passionate concern for spiritual liberation has spawned a variety of movements: Romanticism, Existentialism, Marxism and so on. From time to time brave efforts are made to reconnect Christianity with one or other of these movements. But the gap is now felt to be too wide. Until the sixteenth century Christianity was itself the leading edge, but now it is heteronomous and regressive. Our culture has assigned to Christianity the task of guarding tradition and being the repository of admittedly obsolete but deeply cherished beliefs and images. The church is a museum, and museums are not in the business of pioneering. Thus any attempt to reconnect Christianity with the leading edge of spiritual development must appear naive, incongruous and ridiculous. It is as likely to be mocked within the church as outside it, for the faithful love the museum and most theologians love being scholarly museum curators. There are only a very few dissidents.

The dissidents or heretics are people who, in spite of all that has happened, still hope it might be possible to reconnect religion with modernity.

12

THE TRIUMPH OF THE RELIGIOUS CONSCIOUSNESS

What is religion for? When people engage in the practice of religion what are they hoping to achieve?

The leading religious concepts indicate the answer: religion is about holiness, exaltation, power, lordship, spirituality, autonomy, freedom, knowledge, blessedness, universality and transcendence over nature. The work of religion is to celebrate the triumph of universal, free and sovereign consciousness, emancipated from and lord over nature. That is worship.

And what is it that has all these marvellous qualities and powers? Are they to be ours, or do they belong to another?

The harshest kind of objectifying religious thought sees them all as the exclusive possession of a God whom it sets over against man, for it holds that a human being is neither himself a lord nor destined for lordship, but merely one who needs a Lord. On the realist or objectifying view, religion is rational for two reasons: the first is that God exists and is our Lord, and the second (less often adverted to) is that he has made us for himself so that it suits human nature to be subject to a Lord.

If we pursue this line of thought we find ourselves led to pessimism, to conservatism and finally to scepticism. For, we say to ourselves, it is obviously absurdly presumptuous to suppose that the divine attributes could be for *me*. Even to think such a thing would be to flirt with the sin of Lucifer and to court damnation. So it is a religious duty to project them outwards upon an extraneous deity. By objectification I modestly distance myself from those awesome attributes and can then repudiate any suggestion that I might seek to acquire them. Objectified, they are less chal-

lenging and easier to cope with. Now it is clear that I am not
required to be a star it is safe for me to be a fan, enjoying in the
other a glory that I do not dream could ever be my own. Objectifying religion must regard the fan as the ideal type of believer,
for nobody could be more sincerely disinterested than your true
fan. He is a genuinely unselfish lover. Why, in some cases dead
stars who can no longer bestow even the smallest favour upon
their devotees still have ardent fan clubs. How many dead gods
can say as much for themselves? The fan, a true believer, takes his
own insignificance so completely for granted that he is scarcely
even aware of how deeply he despises himself. He is a nobody and
his highest happiness lies in glorifying one who is somebody, an
act of glorification which is an end in itself. Since he does not
expect to gain anything the fan does not worry that his cult is
profitless.

When the believer's relation to God is like that, pessimism is
close at hand. The believer's disinterestedness is not of the genuinely liberating and religious kind. On the contrary, it is merely an
expression of his conviction of his own utter worthlessness. As he
sees it, a human being is not cut out for autonomy and freedom.
He is fit only to live vicariously as someone else's handmaid, which
is why an unemancipated and subjected woman was traditionally
the ideal type of believer.

Why does he need his Lord so much? The answer given is that
human nature is wayward and wicked, and needs to be disciplined
and controlled. He is not fit to choose and pursue his own goals,
but must be patiently guided towards goals selected for him by one
wiser than he. Without constant supervision he loses his way and
becomes self-destructive.

There is a vision here of a universe in which every being needs
to be tamed and ordered by what is next above it in rank. Wild
animal nature needs to be domesticated, broken and harnessed by
man, and man himself likewise needs to be tamed by God. There
is a certain justice in the whole system. The ship's cat is kicked by
the midshipman, but she has the satisfaction of seeing the midshipman in his turn being kicked by the captain.

Religion is regarded as all the more necessary to society because
of the special nature of human wickedness. If man were merely
wild in the way an animal is, he could doubtless be tamed by a
system of external rewards and punishments. But human wickedness is inward, intractable and irrational. An external policeman
is not enough to secure good behaviour because when they get a

chance people will overthrow him or outwit him. No, the only really effective sanction is the fear of God, the inner policeman that is irremovably installed within everyone who has had a religious upbringing. This inner monitor sees everything, forgets nothing and allows the wicked no peace. There is nowhere to run to from it, and no way of appeasing it except by submission. All merely human administrations leave loopholes which people sooner or later discover and exploit, but God's administration leaves no loopholes.

This conservative view of the function of religion as a dyke against sin, a bridle to restrain human perversity, cannot be faulted for the severity of its pessimism. In effect it is being said that people need very firm government. Merely human systems of totalitarian social control, of the sorts established by twentieth-century dictators, are quite insufficient. God runs an altogether tighter operation. That it works so well is a sort of design-argument for the truth of religion, for the ingenious way religion exploits the structure of the human psyche is a small miracle, like the domestication of the dog. The shepherd's training redirects and exploits the dog's behaviour-patterns so cunningly that the result appears completely natural, as if the animal had been specially created to be a sheepdog. The extraordinary thing about religion is that our aptitude for it is, if anything, even greater than that. They say that around his second birthday a child's aptitude for language is so great that he picks it up as quickly even if his parents are deaf and dumb; and similarly people's aptitude for religion is so great that even a slapdash and crude religious education implants controls that last for life. In each case the aptitude is so great that the pupil appears able to compensate for defects in the teaching. In the former case linguists have been led to speak of a genetically-inbuilt aptitude for language, and in the latter case theologians have said that 'the soul is naturally Christian'.[1]

Maybe: but now we are moving into scepticism. We are beginning to see religion not as intrinsically valuable, but as a means to some other end. And there is an intimate connection between religious objectification, pessimism about human nature, and the use of religion as an instrument of social control. As we have seen, the numinous religious powers and qualities are projected outwards and ascribed to a jealous God who has no intention of parting with them. They are not for us. We must worship from afar and keep to our own modest place in the whole scheme of things. Thus conservatives maintain that the divine attributes are not really communicable to men in this life, and the heresy that established churches regularly punished most severely was the one that claimed that the ordinary person could bypass the religious bureaucracy, enjoy immediate communion with God, and so receive divine charismata at first hand. The conservative's every instinct teaches him that the social order is founded upon religious heteronomy and he smells heresy in any doctrine that promises religious immediacy, be it anabaptism, quakerism, mysticism or methodism. Heresy is not an intellectual mistake: if it were merely *that*, it would be insignificant. Heresy is a threat to society because the religious enthusiast subversively claims for the common man more of religious immediacy than is compatible with the maintenance of the social order.

By the time I have reached this point I no longer have any religion of my own to speak of. I have joined Hobbes and others like him. Religion is a tool for keeping other people in order, and to do that effectively it must be thoroughly heteronomous. Objectification is politics, for we project the divine outwards precisely in order to make religion an efficient control system. Divinity can then only be approached through the proper channels, and by the time it gets down to the man in the pew society ensures that it is very highly diluted. When I understand why this must be so I will no longer pray for myself, for I will not actually and in my own person actively pursue religious ideals or expect to attain the divine attributes. I will have settled instead for what objectified religion offers – resignation, tranquillity and acceptance of one's allotted place in the scheme of things. I have become a churchman, a believer in folk religion, one who attends religious rites in order to contemplate with satisfaction the good that they are doing to others who are my juniors in age or rank.

That is the way religion dies, by a progress through objectification, pessimism and conservatism to scepticism. But suppose that we had from the outset taken the opposite route? After all, God was formerly supposed to be one to whom we could attain. One could imitate God. One could become a partaker of the divine nature. The believer was supposed to become holy as God is holy and righteous as God is righteous, to be filled with the divine spirit and to exercise at least in a delegated way something of the divine sovereignty over nature. Jew as well as Greek supposed there could be some kind of self-communication of God to man. Later theology distinguished between God's incommunicable and communicable attributes, a distinction which we earlier interpreted as separating

the formal features of the religious requirement from the material
content of what is required of us. All this suggests that those divine
attributes of holiness, exaltation, power, lordship, spirituality and
so on could be for us, as spiritual goals that we ought to be
attaining. Admittedly, developed and established Christianity
taught most emphatically that orthodoxy is alienation and true
religion is heteronomy, but there was always an undercurrent to
the opposite effect that might occasionally erupt. According to
Elaine Pagels, for example, the author of the *Gospel of Philip*
criticizes the view that religious language describes external objects.
On the contrary, he says, it is a language of internal transformations. Whoever perceives divine reality becomes what he sees:

> You saw the Spirit, you became spirit.
> You saw Christ, you became Christ. You saw [the
> Father, you] shall become Father. . . . You see
> yourself and what you see you shall [become].[2]

Suppose then that those great qualities and powers, the divine
attributes, are spiritual goals for us to pursue: then we must
straightaway register the fact that the tradition warns us that there
is a right and a wrong way to go about it. The wrong way,
symbolized by Lucifer, snatches at equality with God. The right
way is the way of humility, disinterestedness and self-surrender.
Objectifying religion inevitably misinterprets this distinction for its
own purposes, representing any lofty spiritual aspiration after divine freedom and autonomy as sinful pride, and commending heteronomy, the *sacrificium intellectus*, and docile obedience to church
authority. It is as if Jesus had after all been a Sadducee! This is not
where the true meaning of the distinction lies. The real sin of
Lucifer lies in pursuing divine freedom, knowledge, power and so
on not with a pure heart but with the intention of using them to
bolster a still-unregenerate self. That is futile and potentially evil.
The developed religious consciousness is quite certainly not merely
a stronger, brighter and better-defended version of the natural
human consciousness. On the contrary, it comes to fulfilment only
through renunciation and self-giving. For the traditions of faith are
unanimous that there has to be a mortification of the empirical
self. There must take place what is variously described as a death
and rebirth, a discipline of purgation, a transformation of the self,
and a passage from darkness to light. For there is no way of saving

the empirical self, the ego. It is quite certain to die and be annihilated.

It is a great help at this point to be a religious person who does *not* believe in life after death. People clutch at the thought that there might be, well, just the faintest chance of even a temporary reprieve, to get themselves off the hook. There is no such chance. Death is death.

We need all kinds of devices to force ourselves to think the finality of death. One is to think the deadness of all the people who have said good things about death. Contradicting Plato, Spinoza said that the wise man's meditation is not of death but of life – and now Spinoza is dead. Keynes said that in the long run we are all dead, meaning that all calculation is conditional and we can deal only with the short term. We should not think too far ahead, so draw the curtains, pull your chair to the fire and let us be cosy for a while – but now Keynes is dead.

Another way of imagining the finality of death is modern. We frequently see and hear sound and film recordings of the dead. The voices sound rich and we see the figures moving full of vitality; but the tide of time has ebbed and left them stranded.

The more steadfastly we meditate on the certainty of death, and in particular on the inevitable dissolution of the 'I' behind my eyes, the more clearly we see the only remedy. Quickly we must die to death, escape from the tyranny of this natural ego that clings so hopelessly to life, and enter upon a new and divine form of consciousness, disinterested, universal, non-egoistic and free.

If such a consciousness is attainable then we ought to strive with all our might to attain it. For the wages of death is sin, as St Paul ought to have said. It is the fear of death, the fear of our own abandonment, loss and dissolution that creates the false, fearful, craving ego at the root of our unhappiness. Those who have died to death have attained the highest happiness and can fulfil the moral requirement. They show that religion is rational, not in the sense that religious beliefs correctly portray metaphysical states of affairs, but in the sense that the religious consciousness is the mode of consciousness that offers the highest happiness, is capable of the highest virtue, and is the most appropriate to our condition. The best preparation for death is a state of non-attachment, and there is a good old tradition of saying that in death one finds oneself deprived even of one's faith in God. Objectifying faith is no defence against death, for its objects do not in fact defend us. It will have to be lost *then*, and if it will have to be lost then, then for God's sake let us lose it now! So objectifying belief in God is no defence against death, but to have a divine consciousness is to have conquered the fear of death, for a divine consciousness has renounced and lost that in it which fears death, namely the old ego. And what is the best way of learning this divine consciousness? Strangely enough, it is the discipline of autonomy; for autonomy is disinterestedness. That is to say, the more autonomous I become and the less dependent upon external approval, guidelines and sanctions, the more I find I am obliged to learn to love and to cherish my religious and moral values for their own sakes – that is, disinterestedly. I have to learn disinterested love and prayer and worship and hopefulness, and there is nobody, but nobody, out there who is going to pat me on the back and give me a little reward for my efforts. There will be no small but public presentation ceremony at which I will receive the notice I hunger for. I am on my own, and thus it is that the discipline of autonomy is a discipline of disinterestedness.

And so far as I can learn it, to become fully disinterested in this way is to approximate to the divine consciousness, that is, to draw near to God. For on any account of the matter God is autonomous, free and disinterested and does not seek anyone else's protection and approval; and was it not always said that to draw near to God is to become like God, and to become like God is to draw near to God? So the discipline of transcendence, the hard way of non-attachment, freedom, autonomy and the inwardly-disinterested loving pursuit of religious values – this discipline is the only way to the only God. Just how far I can actually attain to this divine consciousness may be controversial, but at least there can be no doubt that my best hope lies in striving after it.

13

CONCLUSION

A human being is a self-conscious subject emerging from nature and continually striving to enlarge the scope of his consciousness, and with it his freedom. He is a process of becoming. Continually self-dissatisfied and projecting himself forward, he lives habitually several steps ahead of his actual attainment. It is as if he repeatedly throws a grappling-hook upwards and forward, and then drags himself laboriously towards it.

The ultimate goal of this endeavour is the God of religion. In religion we celebrate the triumph of a free, universal, disinterested sovereign consciousness which is spirit because it is wholly autonomous and emancipated from the constraints of natural necessity. It is lord over nature, holy, exalted, lucid, self-possessed, blissful and unlimited in its range.

We know that we fall infinitely short of this ideal that we celebrate. A lower stage of consciousness, though it may aspire after a higher, never fully understands it, otherwise it would already possess it. Each step forward in the spiritual life requires one to leave behind something easy, known and familiar, and to receive as if it were a grace something that is as yet fearful and unknown. The process is one of continual mortification, self-surrender and purging while yet at the same time, and paradoxically, it is also a movement towards greater autonomy and self-possession. God is projected as the absolute religious ideal that altogether surpasses our understanding. He is what is ultimately required of us. We have to move towards him and to become progressively more like him, until we are completely united with him and possess his attributes. At that ideal limit he is ours and we are his, but one may not ever claim actually to have reached that point. For one thing, human nature is too ambiguous for one to be able to make confident claims about progress in the spiritual life; and for another, if one did reach the ideal then aspiration would cease and so life would cease. So the ideal is elusive: it is approached not head-on but indirectly, and it is not seized but surrendered to.

From this peculiar character of the self's journey towards salvation arises the familiar paradoxical language of the spiritual life. Since each progressively larger and more liberated stage of religious consciousness is mysterious to the one before it, the whole journey is experienced as a movement into unknowing. I gain sovereignty by self-surrender, riches through poverty, strength through weakness, and an immortal, universal and disinterested self by dying to the self.

The main interest of religion is in the conquest of evil by the transformation of the self. We seek to escape from a self that is mean, narrow, darkened, acquisitive, trapped in the world and terrified of death, and we seek to become autonomous, free, creative, universally-loving and disinterested spirit that has gained release from bondage to sin and death. The emancipation of consciousness that religion seeks makes possible, and gives worth and stability to, all the other concerns of civilization such as science and art. Indeed, without the progressive religious development of consciousness no lasting happiness is attainable at all.

God is the pearl of great price, the treasure hidden at the centre of the religious life. The religious claim and demand upon us is God's will, the drama of the religious life within us is God's activity, and the goal of the religious life before us is God's nature. But we should not suppose God to be a substance, an independently-existing being who can be spoken of in a descriptive and non-religious way. Religious language is not in the business of describing really-existing super-sensible objects and their activities. We do not nowadays have sufficient reason to suppose that there are any such beings or influences, and in any case religion is not concerned with them. No external object can bring about my inner spiritual liberation. I must will it for myself and attain it within myself. Only I can free myself. So the religious imperative that commands me to become spirit must be regarded as an autonomously-authoritative principle that I impose upon myself. I internalize it as a principle that commands me to seek the religious ideal. I freely choose to pursue religious goals. It follows that religious language is not descriptive or metaphysical but intensely practical. It is used in order to provoke and to prompt change within the self. That purpose can be achieved in many ways – by threat and admonition, by parable and satire, by exhortation and promise, and so forth. The linguistic forms used by the biblical teachers, and above all by Jesus, are extraordinarily varied. Their common feature is that they are not concerned with quasi-scientific description, but with bringing about religious change in the hearer. The teacher's language rings an alarm bell, applies a goad, tears down a barrier to self-knowledge and so on. Correspondingly, religious language used confessionally by the believer expresses contrition, repentance, aspiration, thanksgiving and so forth. The teacher's language is concerned to evoke religious change, and the believer's language expresses what it is to undergo religious change, but neither of them is concerned with describing metaphysical entities.

Faith, then, is a matter of the will. Faith is not created by arguments designed to show that certain metaphysical dogmas are true, but by a use of language that cuts us to the heart, shows us that we have been dull and blind, and persuades us to start taking religion seriously.

How far can religion be understood and communicated in an objective and impartial manner? The various visible and institutional aspects of religion are obviously part of history and just as accessible to historical understanding as anything else that falls under the purview of the historian. But religion in the sense of a personal faith is more controversial. On the popular realist view, the religious believer is one who assents to and acts upon a body of religious doctrines. These religious doctrines are picturesque and remarkable metaphysical claims about supernatural beings, their activities, their dealings with mankind and so forth. The Apostles' Creed, for example, may be thought to imply a body of such supernatural doctrines. Realists think that there is a body of doctrines, the Faith that is believed, which can be *understood* in a religiously-neutral way; there is *assent* to this body of doctrines; and there is fiduciary *trust*, faith the virtue of acting upon and being loyal to the Faith believed. The three distinct mental acts were traditionally called *notitia, assensus* and *fiducia* respectively.

Now if realism is correct there is no special problem about understanding religion, and no need for special linguistic techniques for communicating it. Quite the opposite: faith is simple, for a religion consists of nothing but a set of assertions which may be highly improbable but are not elusive or obscure. On the contrary, they are claimed to be publicly accessible and readily intelligible. So one can teach all that is in religion in an impartial and purely descriptive way, leaving people free to decide for themselves whether or not to assent – upon authority – to a particular religious belief-system.

There can be no doubt that many people do understand religion in this way, and since it is widely held that meanings are publicly-determined and that popular usage is the final arbiter, the religious realists think their own position secure. But where religious truth is concerned it is not sufficient to accept the verdict of ordinary language and common convention. Religious truth is subjectivity. I must learn in myself how religious example and utterance can shake and challenge my ordinary self-understanding. I must myself undergo inner change. Realism suggests that it is enough to assent to a set of propositions and to act as one who sincerely believes them true; but it is not. One must become subjective.

We have conducted a long campaign against theological realism, and in the course of it have taken leave of the God of metaphysical theism. We have sought to describe instead a modern and fully-autonomous spirituality, which may claim to be the legitimate successor of earlier Christian spiritualities.

I continue to speak of God and to pray to God. God is the mythical embodiment of all that one is concerned with in the spiritual life. He is the religious demand and ideal, the pearl of great price and the enshriner of values. He is needed – but as a myth.

We need myth because we are persons. A person is a process of becoming, and narrative is the literary form that best shows what persons are and can become. Persons all have life-stories, and indeed you might say that a person just is a story. Now the religious life is an inner drama, the story of our response to the eternal religious requirement. It must be expressed in story-form, and religious stories are myths. Myth is the best, clearest and most effective way of communicating religious truth.

God is a myth we have to have. What is new in modern times is that the advance of consciousness has compelled us to admit the mythological character of much of our own religious – and also metaphysical – thinking. Metaphysical and religious belief-systems are works of human art and the vehicles of cherished spiritual values and intuitions. It is not an altogether easy admission to make, but it is forced upon us and once we have made it there is no going back. We have to go forward to a new kind of faith

which is fully conscious. It uses myth, but it also transcends it into
autonomy.

> self government
> independence

↓ does he describe autonomy?
  (check)
    — what are the advantages
      & disadvantages of autonomy?

— pt p.47. asking people to do
what a highly rel. person has
experienced — is this possible?
If it is a faith — how
will one arrive at it?

Notes

1 Introductory

1. Recent literature on Providence is reviewed by M. F. Wiles, 'Religious Authority and Divine Action', *Working Papers in Doctrine*, SCM Press 1976, pp. 132–147; and Brian L. Hebblethwaite, 'Providence and Divine Action', *Religious Studies* 14, 1978, pp. 223–236; 'Some Reflections on Predestination, Providence and Divine Foreknowledge', *Religious Studies* 15, 1979, pp. 433–448.

2. Kierkegaard, *Purity of Heart is to Will One Thing*, 1847; tr. D. V. Steere, New York, Harper Torchbooks 1956, is particularly striking.

2 The Decline of Objective Theism

1. Julian Jaynes, *The Origin of Consciousness in the Breakdown of the Bicameral Mind*, Allen Lane 1979.

2. Ernest Gellner, *Legitimation of Belief*, Cambridge University Press 1974, p. 173.

3. Charles Taylor, *Hegel*, Cambridge University Press 1975, ch. 1 and passim, has an admirable account of the emergence of the modern self-understanding.

4. I owe this very brief and neat way of explaining the slogan that 'existence is not a predicate' to Alvin Plantinga.

5. Augustine, *Soliloquies*, 2, 1, 1.

6. On theism and explanation, see Keith Ward, *The Concept of God*, Blackwell 1974, ch. 8, §§3–8.

7. Norman Malcolm, 'Anselm's Ontological Arguments,' *Philosophical Review* 69, 1960, pp. 41–62.

8. David Hume, *Dialogues Concerning Natural Religion*, 1779, Part V.

3 The Charge of Reductionism

1. Alasdair MacIntyre, 'God and the Theologians', *Encounter*, September 1963; reprinted with a reply by Robinson in John A. T. Robinson and D. L. Edwards, *The Honest to God Debate*, SCM Press 1963, pp. 222f.

2. John A. T. Robinson, *The New Reformation?*, SCM Press 1965, Appendix I.

3. Robinson, *The Human Face of God*, SCM Press 1973, p. 22.

4. R. W. Hepburn *Christianity and Paradox*, Watts 1959; 'A Critique of Humanist Theology', in H. J. Blackham (ed.), *Objections to Humanism*, Constable 1963, pp. 29–54; and other writings.

5. Roger Trigg, *Reason and Commitment*, Cambridge University Press 1973, pp. 78–81.

6. F. D. Maurice, *Theological Essays*, Macmillan 1853, VIII.

7. Anthony Flew and Alasdair MacIntyre (eds), *New Essays in Philosophical Theology*, SCM Press 1955, p. 230.

8. Ibid., p. 233.

9. Ibid.

10. Ibid., p. 234.

11. This point is argued in great detail in W. Cantwell Smith, *The Meaning and End of Religion*, New York: Macmillan 1962, SPCK 1978.

4 Creation and Theological Realism

1. Mircea Eliade, *Patterns in Comparative Religion*, Sheed & Ward 1958, ch. II.

2. From 'Faith in God the Creator' (1934) tr. Schubert M. Ogden in *Existence and Faith*, Hodder & Stoughton 1961, p. 176.

3. Ibid., p. 181.

4. Irenaeus, *adv. Haer.*, 2, 1, 4f.

5. Philaret of Moscow (1782–1867); cited in V. Lossky, *The Mystical Theology of the Eastern Church*, James Clarke 1957, p. 92.

6. Origen, *De Oratione*, Books. V, VI.

7. S. Kierkegaard, *Journals* X^5 A 72 (January 1853); No. 1287 in the selection edited by A. Dru, Oxford 1938.

5 Worship and Theological Realism

1. The two points of view meet and collide in Stuart C. Brown (ed.), *Reason and Religion*, Cornell University Press 1977. For a sympathetic appraisal of one of the leading 'expressivists', D. Z. Phillips, see Alan Keightley, *Wittgenstein, Grammar and God*, Epworth Press 1976.

2. Kierkegaard, *Fear and Trembling*, Copenhagen 1843; tr. W. Lowrie, Princeton University Press 1941.

3. E.g., *The Future of an Illusion*, Hogarth Press 1928, especially ch. VI.

4. Ninian Smart, *The Concept of Worship*, Macmillan 1972.

5. *The Essence of Christianity* was published in 1841; *The Sickness unto Death* appeared in 1849.

6. *The Sickness unto Death*. Part First, III, A, (b), (2): Lowrie translation, New York: Doubleday 1954, pp. 173f.

7. Ibid., pp. 146f.

8. Kierkegaard, *Works of Love*, 1847, Part Two, ch. IX.

9. D. Z. Phillips, *Death and Immortality*, Macmillan 1970, passim.

6 Doctrine and Disinterestedness

1. E.g., Cicero, *De Natura Deorum*, II, 45–59.
2. E.g., R. G. Swinburne, *The Coherence of Theism*, Oxford University Press 1977.
3. E.g., Anthony Kenny, *The God of the Philosophers*, Oxford University Press 1979.
4. Ibid., p. 128.
5. Ibid., p. 127.
6. Session VI, on Justification (January 1547). The classical discussion of the issues is K. E. Kirk, *The Vision of God*, Longmans 1931, pp. 415–472.
7. A point particularly emphasized in the writings of Wilfred Cantwell Smith: e.g. *The Meaning and End of Religion*, New York: Macmillan 1963 and SPCK 1978; *Faith and Belief*, Princeton 1979.
8. For example in *Explorations in Theology 5*, SCM Press 1979, passim.

7 The Meaning of God

1. Anthony Kenny, *The God of the Philosophers*, Oxford University Press 1979, p. 10.
2. Ibid., p. 6.
3. See Alan Keightley, *Wittgenstein, Grammar and God*, Epworth Press 1976, especially pp. 122ff.

8 How Real Should God Be?

1. For an example of such a cosmic supermind see the novel by Fred Hoyle, *The Black Cloud*, Penguin Books 1960.
2. The story is of course from Kierkegaard. My memory has somewhat altered the original, to be found in the great Address on 'The Unchangeableness of God'. See *For Self-Examination and Judge for Yourselves!*, tr. Walter Lowrie, Oxford 1946, pp. 232 ff.
3. C. C. Gillispie, *Genesis and Geology*, New York: Harper Torchbooks 1959, passim.

9 Is the Religious Ideal Attainable?

1. David Hume, *The Natural History of Religion*, 1757, ch. IX ff.
2. Studdert-Kennedy, op. cit., pp. 10, 95.
3. Don Cupitt, *Jesus and the Gospel of God*, Lutterworth Press 1979, passim.
4. Michael Argyle and Benjamin Beit-Hallahmi, *The Social Psychology of Religion*, Routledge & Kegan Paul 1975, pp. 136 ff.

10 Faith as an Act of the Will

1. S. Kierkegaard, *Journals*, selected, edited and translated by Alexander Dru, Oxford University Press 1938, no. 1021 on p. 355 (= X^2 A 299).

2. For an authoritative judgment on just how much Kant concedes at this point, see Lewis White Beck, *A Commentary on Kant's Critique of Practical Reason*, University of Chicago Press, Phoenix edition 1963, p. 263 and no. 8.

3. Wilfred Cantwell Smith, *Belief and History*, Charlottesville: University Press of Virginia 1977; *Faith and Belief*, Princeton University Press 1979. These two books are to be used, I think, with some caution, but they contain a great deal of valuable evidence.

4. E.g., John Burnaby, 'Christian Prayer', *Soundings*, ed. A. R. Vidler, Cambridge University Press 1962.

5. William Canton, *The Invisible Playmate*, 1894, subsequently reprinted in Everyman's Library no. 566 and exceedingly sentimental, I must confess.

6. See St John's drawing of Mount Carmel in Gerald Brennan, *St John of the Cross*, Cambridge University Press 1973, Plate 4.

11 The Justification of Faith

1. John Rawls, *A Theory of Justice*, Oxford University Press 1972.

2. Paul Hazard, *The European Mind 1680–1715*, ET first published 1953, reprinted Penguin Books 1973.

12 The Triumph of the Religious Consciousness

1. Tertullian, *Apology*, xvii.

2. *Gospel of Philip* 61, 29–35; cited in Elaine Pagels, *The Gnostic Gospels*, Weidenfeld & Nicolson 1980, p. 134.

Index of Names

Aquinas, Thomas, 24ff., 33, 38, 99
Anselm, 21ff., 32
Argyle, M., 170
Aristotle, 89
Arnold, Matthew, 127
Augustine, 21ff., 102, 168

Barth, Karl, 7
Beck, L. W., 171
Beit-Hallahmi, B., 170
Blackham, H. J., 169
Brennan, G., 171
Brown, S. C., 169
Bultmann, R., 41ff., 49f.
Burnaby, J., 171

Calvin, John, 102
Canton, William, 171
Cicero, 170
Cupitt, Don, 170

Darwin, Charles, 28
Dostoevsky, F., 113
Durkheim, E., 16

Edwards, D. L., 168
Eliade, M., 169

Feuerbach, L., 16, 64f.
Fichte, J., 21
Filmer, Robert, 19
Flew, Anthony G. N., 169
Freud, S., 16, 59f.

Gellner, E., 16, 168
Gillispie, C. C., 170

Hazard, Paul, 171
Hebblethwaite, B. L., 168
Hegel, G. W. F., 10f., 21, 66f., 75, 120f.
Hepburn, R. W., 37, 41f., 169
Homer, 63
Hoyle, F., 170
Hume, David, 33, 106, 108, 168, 170

Irenaeus, St, 169

James, William, 79
Jaynes, Julian, 16, 168
John of the Cross, St, 138f.
Jung, C. G., 7f., 89

Kafka, Franz, 113
Kant, I., 4, 8, 21, 67f., 100, 127, 143, 146f., 171
Keightley, Alan W., 169
Kenny, Anthony, 75, 170
Keynes, J. M., 161
Kierkegaard, S., 7f., 59, 64ff., 75, 92, 113f., 117, 127, 168ff.
Kirk, K. E., 170
Küng, Hans, 129

Leibniz, G. W., 26, 106
Locke, John, 19
Lossky, Vladimir, 169
Lowrie, Walter, 169
Luther, Martin, 7, 92

MacIntyre, Alasdair C., 35, 168f.
MacKinnon, Donald M., 79f.

Malcolm, Norman, 33, 168
Marx, Karl, 16
Maurice, F. D., 40, 169
Miles, T. R., 34
Milton, John, 151
Montaigne, M. de, 81

Newman, J. H., 102

Ogden, Schubert M., 169
Origen, 169

Pagels, Elaine, 160, 171
Paley, William, 28, 124
Parmenides, 73
Pascal, Blaise, 7
Philaret, 51, 169
Phillips, D. Z., 34, 69, 169
Philo, 7f., 84
Plantinga, Alvin, 168
Plato, 145, 161

Ramsey, I. T., 38
Rawls, John, 145, 171

Robinson, John A. T., 8, 35ff., 43,
   168f.

Schleiermacher, F. D. E., 35
Smart, R. Ninian, 34, 60, 169
Smith, W. Cantwell, 169ff.
Spinoza, B. de, 73, 106, 161
Steere, D. V., 168
Studdert-Kennedy, G. A.,
   112, 170
Swinburne, R. G., 170

Taylor, Charles, 168
Tertullian, 7, 171
Tolstoy, Leo, 113
Trigg, Roger, 38, 169

Van Gogh, Vincent, 30
Vidler, A. R., 171
Voltaire, 106

Weil, Simone, 113, 117
Wiles, M. F., 168
Wittgenstein, L., 33, 113.

– can have faith without any doctrine at all..?

– have faith without trust?

reductionism — n. any method or theory of reducing data, processes, or statements to seeming equivalents that are less complex or developed; usually a disparaging term

subjectivism — the philosophic theory that all knowledge is subjective & relative, never objective ... ③ an ethical theory holding that personal attitudes & feelings are the sole determinants of moral & aesthetic values.

aberration

deleterious (P 40)

fiduciary p(165)

expressivists p87 (Don Cupitt)

apotropaic p.59

anthropomorphic — (adj.)
anthropomorphism — the attributing
of human shape or characteristic
to a god, animal, or inanimate th

ubiquitous — p.71 present, or
seeming to be present, everywhere
at the same time; omnipresent.
                                    (syn.)

theophany p.85.

heteronomy (n.) p.91

patripassian p112

heterodoxy — p125
heterodox — departing from or opposed
to the usual beliefs or established —
doctrines, esp, in religion; inclining
toward heresy; unorthodox

<u>atheism</u> — a person who believes
that there is no God.
— rejects all rel. beliefs

<u>teleology</u> — the study of final
causes ② the fact or quality of
being directed towards a definite
end or of having an ultimate
purpose, esp. as attributed to
natural processes, 3...

<u>heuristic</u> — helping to discover or
learn; specif., designating a method
of education or of computer program-
ming in which the pupil or machine
proceeds along empirical lines,
using rules of thumb, to find
solutions or answers.

<u>heteronomous</u> — ① subject to
another's laws or rules ②...

<u>faith</u> — ①. unquestioning belief that
does not require proof or evidence.
② unquestioning belief in God,
religious tenets, etc.   p87 conclusion
creeds,

DATE DUE

AUGUSTANA UNIVERSITY COLLEGE
LIBRARY